Contents

Introduction 4

Chapter 1: **Though Unseen, the Lord Is Present** 6

Chapter 2: **The Lord Walks Beside Me** 38

Chapter 3: **The Lord Always Helps Me** 70

Chapter 4: **God Is Truly Faithful** 102

Chapter 5: **Cherished Child** 134

Chapter 6: **The Lord Will Never Leave Me** 166

Chapter 7: **God Carries Me Through Trials** 198

Chapter 8: **Pray Even in the Midst of Doubts** 230

Chapter 9: **The Lord Understands Our Suffering** 262

Chapter 10: **The Lord Strengthens Our Faith** 294

Chapter 11: **God Always Keeps His Promises** 326

Chapter 12: **The Lord Cares for Us** 358

A Journey with God

The idea of taking a journey is a wonderful biblical metaphor for our life experience. We readily relate to the psalmist's description of the Good Shepherd leading us to green pastures and beside still waters, guiding us in paths of righteousness. But then there is that dark valley where the shadow of death lingers and where our doubts may rise up and our fears may threaten our faith. We hesitate there, and sometimes we falter. We may wonder, How could the psalmist declare at such times, "I will fear no evil"?

But long journeys have good and bad, easy and difficult — and long periods of in-between. This book poignantly probes that aspect of changeability during our full life's journey. In a spirit of perplexed wonder, this text seeks to understand the parts of the path that don't make sense, where it seems as if God has forgotten to be good and faithful as he promised to be. During these hard times, what is missing, and what can you try to get back through a sustained relationship with God?

When your life has been at its darkest, and your journey has been most frustrating and painful, have you ever wondered or even shouted in anger, "God, where are you?!" It is a question for the ages. It is a question that points to our deepest longings. It holds our greatest fear, our most profound need, and even our highest hope. Why didn't the psalmist fear? Why in that valley of the shadow of death did he feel safe and sure? The reason he gives is summed up in five profound words of faith: "For you are with me." He believed that, even in the worst times, God really was there.

Journeys of Faith is a stepping stone to developing a deeper trust in God's abiding presence through thick and thin. Right now the bumps in the road may still trip us up, the disappointments may sometimes make us stumble, and our pain may cause us to question God's goodness and love. But as we continue on the journey, seeking to walk with God, our faith is sure to become stronger each day of our lives.

In fact, the day-to-day nature of life's journey is the subject of this prayer book. It helps you hold your relationship with God close to your heart when it is easy as well as difficult. It also reminds you that God is with you and loves you no matter what.

Prayers contained in *Journeys of Faith* are written as honest, heartfelt dialogue with God. In fact, you're likely to hear the echoes of your own struggles in them, as well as encouragement that will foster your growing faith in God's love for you. As you make your way through these pages, you will find yourself with renewed and rejuvenated faith.

Chapter 1

Though Unseen, the Lord Is Present

Dear Lord, I sometimes feel as if you don't hear me, or see me, or care about me. I feel lost even when I call out to you, for it seems as though you do not answer me. I pray for the discernment of your Holy Spirit. I know you are always there, but when my faith wavers, I find myself looking to outside things for proof, and yet I know that the proof of you exists in my heart. Please help me remember that yours is a quiet presence that does not shout or attract attention or use big gestures to make yourself known. Help me remember that you are always at my side and that what my eyes cannot see, my heart truly can. Amen.

JOURNEYS OF
Faith

Publications International, Ltd.

$\mathcal{H}$oly God, your constant and ever-present love is my strength and my foundation. When all around me falls to pieces, I know that with your Spirit to guide me, I can put those pieces back together and be stronger than ever before. You are the wind that allows me to soar and the breath that gives me life. Though I never see your face, I see your countenance upon the smiles of my friends, in the laughter of my children, and throughout the challenges and miracles that occur each day. I need nothing else than to know that you never leave me and that you live within my heart, my soul, and my spirit. Thank you, God

> *Beneath the touch of a helping hand, we can feel God's strong grasp. If we hold on, we are no longer alone.*

Heavenly Father, reach out to me today with the touch of your presence. I am anxious about many things that I will have to face this day. I long to know that I am not alone and that you will be right here with me to guide me to the right actions and decisions that are the highest and best for all concerned. Let me feel the soft push of your loving hands as you gently direct my steps, and I will open my heart to listen to the whispers of wisdom you have for me and for my situation today. Touch my spirit with yours, and lead me to better days ahead. Amen.

My Lord and Savior, are you here for me today? I can't feel your presence, and my lack of faith and trust is getting the better of me right now. Please help me move beyond fear and doubt and know that you are always here and always ready to be my rock and my foundation. My human qualities sometimes keep me from being reminded of my constant connection to you, and I ask that you remind me once again of that connection, as I rise to face the day. Thank you, Lord.

Every valley shall be exalted, and every mountain and hill shall be made low: and the crooked shall be made straight, and the rough places plain. And the glory of the Lord shall be revealed, and all flesh shall see it together: for the mouth of the Lord hath spoken it.
— Isaiah 40:4–5

When the world around us grows cold and chaotic, faith is the balm that soothes a fearful heart and the blanket that comforts an anxious mind.

Almighty God, your love is like a pair of invisible arms that hold me up when I am about to fall and lift me up when I am down. My faith assures me that your presence is the eternal grace that I can always count on to carry me when my own strength is simply not enough. I may not see you standing there behind me, but my heart hears your voice telling me I am never alone. Your love is like a pair of invisible wings upon which I can soar above the challenges and problems of the day.

$\mathcal{H}$oly God, are you here with me? It's me again, asking for your direction and guidance. Bless me with your mercy and grace that I may do the right thing and say the right thing in every situation I encounter. With you as my constant companion, my everlasting Father, I know that my words and deeds shall be your will and not mine, for my will is often not the best choice. I ask for your wise council today and every day and that you forever remain at my side. Thanks be to you, God.

> $\mathcal{T}$he Lord thy God in the midst of thee is mighty; he will save, he will rejoice over thee with joy; he will rest in his love, he will joy over thee with singing.
> — Zephaniah 3:17

*D*ear God, I don't thank you often enough for the miracles you work in my life each and every day. They may not always be big spectacular miracles, but even the small-est reminders of your presence serve to make my heart sing and my spirit soar. Thank you for always being here, no mat-ter how badly I screw up or what dumb mistakes I make in the course of my life. You never judge nor condemn, and you are quick to forgive and show mercy. Thank you for being the loving God that you are, even when it takes every ounce of my faith to believe that you are here with me.

Heavenly Father, here I am before you, asking for your loving care. My faith in you is what gets me through the trying times in life, and your constant presence keeps the flame of hope alive in my heart when the darkness threatens to surround me. Shower me with your mercy, that I may be made stronger and more resilient in the wake of your love and attention. So please take my hands and pull me up and onto my feet, ready to walk the path you have set out before me. I have faith in you, Holy Father, now and forever. In Jesus' name, I pray. Amen.

When you close your doors, and make darkness within, remember never to say that you are alone, for you are not alone; nay, God is within. — Epictetus

O Lord, why do I always have to see something to believe in it? I know that you are not something I can see, hear, or touch, and yet you are in everything I see, everything I hear, and everything I touch. Your Spirit confirms for me the power of faith — of believing in what cannot be seen. Your power in my life to heal and

forgive confirms for me that you deeply love me and reveal your love in the people who care for me, in the wonder of nature, in the laughter of a young child, and in the grateful sounds of my pet. Your presence permeates my life, dear Lord, even if I cannot look into your eyes. I am truly blessed with your presence in my life.

In you, dear God, I place my faith. In your presence I find the courage I need to face any challenge and the fortitude I need to overcome any obstacle. Your unseen presence is the force of love in my life that keeps me on the path you have set out before me, unwavering in my devotion to you and the divine plan you have ordained for me. Though you cannot be seen with physical eyes, I see you in every blessing of my life, as well as the tougher times that make me stronger and more resilient. I place my faith in you, and I pray in the name of your most precious Son, Jesus. Amen.

> *If ye have faith as a grain of mustard seed, ye shall say unto this mountain, Remove hence to yonder place; and it shall remove; and nothing shall be impossible unto you.* — Matthew 17:20

Almighty God, I sometimes feel abandoned and alone, as if you have left me and forgotten me. But then something happens, some small miracle or mercy that reminds me that I am never forgotten. Maybe my life continues to be challenging, but I can feel you holding my hand and carrying me when I am faltering under the weight of my fear and doubt. Your footprints in the sand of my life serve to remind me that no matter how dark the night, no matter how difficult the days, you are here ready to take my burdens and carry me to better days ahead. Thank you for being the loving God that you are, even when it takes every ounce of my faith to believe that you are here with me.

$\mathcal{F}$ather in heaven, it's a new day and a new opportunity for me to do your loving work in the world. So please, Lord God, let me be a mirror of your love and compassion to others. You never fail me, even when I am low on faith and trust. You never leave me, even when I look around my life and feel that you have abandoned me. I know that you are always here for me, and I want to go and be there for others and be an unseen and invisible force for love for good — that is, for you. Amen.

*D*ear Lord, the storms of my life often threaten to blow me away, and I feel small and weak and insignificant. Let me hear that still, small voice within that reminds me you are always with me, keeping me safe even as the cold winds blow and even as the hard rains fall. Let me feel the warmth of your ever-present love when life chills me to the bone and while I seek comfort in the shelter of a safe harbor.

> *For ye were sometimes darkness, but now are ye light in the Lord: walk as children of light. For the fruit of the Spirit is in all goodness and righteousness and truth.* — Ephesians 5:8–9

My supreme Lord, your love alone is all I need to get through each day and night, and your grace is my salvation. I need not focus on the things happening outside of me, but on the strength inside me that is your presence. You are my light; like the beacon of a lighthouse you lead me to safe shores. You are my sun that warms the ice I stumble upon, making my path easier to travel. You fill my heart with your mercy, dear God, and I thank you for your presence in my life.

God, whom or what shall I fear when you walk beside me? Nothing can disturb the inner peace that comes from knowing that I'm not alone. No matter how lonely I may feel on the outside, I have a friend, a confidante, a cheerleader, a supporter, and, most of all, a loving Father. You are always here for me, and all I have to do is pray to you, for you are all those things to me. You have never failed me, God, and I hope that I can be more perfect in your eyes as I follow your guidance and live your loving will in my life. Why should I be afraid? I have you, God, as my partner. Thank you.

Even in the face of struggles and difficulties, there is a higher order of goodness at work in our lives. We may not be able to physically detect it at all times, but our faith knows the truth, and the truth sets us free.

I sought the Lord, and he heard me, and delivered
me from all my fears. They looked unto him, and
were lightened: and their faces were not ashamed.
This poor man cried, and the Lord heard him, and
saved him out of all his troubles.

— Psalm 34:4–6

> *The wind bloweth where it listeth, and thou hearest the sound thereof, but canst not tell whence it cometh, and whither it goeth: so is every one that is born of the Spirit.* — John 3:8

Dear God, my body feels tired and weak today. I'm not feeling well, and I need to know that you are here with me, making me stronger just by your presence alone. Knowing that you will never give me more than I can handle helps me understand that there is a reason for what I'm going through, and it makes the challenges somewhat easier. Your will may be mysterious, but I know that your love is real. I rely on you, God, for my physical strength and my spiritual strength as well. Thank you, God.

O Lord, reach out to me and give me your silent strength today. I'm unable to do this on my own, and I know that with you supporting me, nothing will be impossible to overcome. You are my rock and my cornerstone. You are the guiding force in my life that moves through my heart and my soul like a gentle and comforting breeze. Reach out to me today and let me know that I can, and that I will, persevere with your help. Thank you, Lord, for always caring for me and for never abandoning me. Amen.

And he said unto his disciples, Therefore I say unto you, Take no thought for your life, what ye shall eat; neither for the body, what ye shall put on. The life is more than meat, and the body is more than raiment.
— Luke 12:22–23

My Lord, come walk with me today. I need a friend, and you have never forsaken me. Come speak in your still, sweet voice so that my soul may find answers to the questions that I alone cannot find. Come stay with me through each challenge, and celebrate with me the blessings that greet me along the way. My faith in you is strong, and my belief in your love unwavering. Come walk with me today, Lord, as you have walked with me each day before this.

Storms sometimes arrive in our lives with hurricane-force winds. We feel as if our hearts are caught in the vortex. But just when we think we'll be destroyed, a still, small voice appears in the eye of the storm to remind us that we are not alone.

$\mathcal{M}$y God, I am not always good at believing in what my eyes cannot see and what
my senses cannot discern, but I know that
you are everywhere in my life. I look around at
all the blessings I have, and my heart is filled
with gratitude for the gifts you have chosen to
give me. I look around at the trials you have
asked me to undertake, and I realize that you
are my teacher as well as my friend. I do not
have to see you to believe in you, just as you
have always believed in me. Thank you, God,
for opening the eyes of my heart.

What is grace, God? It is the love I feel when I know you are with me, walking beside me and offering me guidance and wisdom. What is faith, God? It is my belief in you, even if I cannot hold your hand or see your face. What is hope, God? It is the joy within my heart when I realize that I can overcome any challenge as long as you are with me. What is love, God? It is you and the blessings you give me.

> *He that cometh from above is above all: he that is of the earth is earthly, and speaketh of the earth: he that cometh from heaven is above all.* — John 3:31

Dear Lord, the flame of hope within my heart is dying, and I ask for you to renew my faith and restore my strength. I know that you are here, watching over me, but right now I need a little extra guidance and encouragement. Like a child who needs her blanket, I ask to be wrapped in your loving care so that the flame of hope is rekindled and burns bright within me again. Renew me, Lord; renew my hope and my faith. Amen.

$\mathcal{G}$od, you have always been faithful and true. You have never failed to be here for me, and you have never failed to help me learn the lessons brought by both my struggles and blessings. I place my entire trust in you, knowing that you will never lead me astray and never abandon me even when others in my life consider me down for the count. Yes, you have blessed me with wonderful friends and family, but I place my faith in you alone, for your power and your presence transcend all things seen and all things unseen. You are a mighty and wonderful God, and my faith is my gift to you.

> *Blessed be ye poor: for yours is the king-dom of God. Blessed are ye that hunger now: for ye shall be filled. Blessed are ye that weep now: for ye shall laugh.* — Luke 6:20–21

Let the truth of your loving presence set me free, dear God, of the fears and worries of this day. Let the truth of your divine mercy set me free from the doubts and anxieties I feel as I meet each new challenge. Let the truth of your forgiveness be the soothing balm that restores my relationships with those I love. You alone are the truth, dear God. You are the higher force in my life, bringing order to the chaos of my spirit. Let the truth set me free, dear God.

$\mathcal{F}$ather in heaven, how can I sleep with this worry and fear keeping me awake all night? Bring me the peace only you can provide — the peace that passes all understanding and calms the stormy seas in my soul. I have done all I can do today, and I ask that you help me with those things I cannot control. Your presence, although unseen, is a constant in my life, and right now, I need that constant presence to remind me that even as I lay my head to rest, you remain awake and alert, watching over me, protecting me, and loving me.

*T*here but for the grace of you, God, go I. Protected by this unseen force that is made up of your love for me and my faith in you. Comforted by this unseen warmth that envelops me and keeps me from suffering through the coldest nights. Guided by this unseen whisper that tells me where to go, what to say, and what to do when my own mind is in too much turmoil to think and my heart is too hurt to feel. There but for the grace of you, God, go I. I am blessed. I am loved. I am grateful. Thank you, God. I pray in Jesus' precious name. Amen.

> *Have courage for the great sorrows of life and patience for the small ones; and when you have laboriously accomplished your daily task, go to sleep in peace. God is awake.* — Victor Hugo

Chapter 2

The Lord Walks Beside Me

O heavenly Father, even on a short journey it's one thing to have a map and an entirely different thing — a far better and more assuring thing — to have a guide. Thank you for being my guide in this lifelong journey, for taking up the road with me and giving me the benefit of your wisdom and the pleasure of your company along the way. I would be lost and lonely without you, but because you walk with me, I am confident and content.

The Lord is on my side; I will not fear: what can man do unto me? The Lord taketh my part with them that help me: therefore shall I see my desire upon them that hate me. It is better to trust in the Lord than to put confidence in man.

— Psalm 118:6–8

Lord Jesus, sometimes I feel as if you can't possibly see my circumstances, because I have difficulty believing it would be your will for me to go through such dark times, times during which I feel isolated, defeated, and without recourse. But then I hear your still, small voice reminding me that I'm not alone, that you are in control, and that your will does not center in circumstances. Rather, your will is rooted in your perfect love for me, and its purpose is to develop the kind of character I need to enjoy a meaningful life and have a deep fellowship with you. Thank you for drawing near to me and encouraging me today.

$\mathcal{A}$long this path of life, Lord Jesus, I've come to realize that no person can be to me what you are. There is a wide spectrum of disappointment I have experienced at the hands of others (including disappointments with myself). Some letdowns have been inadvertent and easy to forgive. Others have been intentional and mean-spirited, and I have struggled to leave these deeper hurts in your hands. But with you, Lord, there is perfect love and support, pure mercy and forgiveness. You are my source of unfailing companionship, and I'm deeply grateful that you walk beside me.

𝒩evertheless I am continually with thee: thou hast holden me by my right hand. Thou shalt guide me with thy counsel, and afterward receive me to glory. Whom have I in heaven but thee? and there is none upon earth that I desire beside thee. — Psalm 73:23–25

Thank you, my supreme Lord, for the gift of prayer — the gift of being able to talk with you and the ability to sense your listening and responding through your Spirit and your Word. Thank you, too, for the people you've placed in my life who express your love to me in practical, tangible ways. By these gifts from your hand, I experience comfort both within and without. By these precious provisions, I know you love me and walk beside me.

Exhausted from walking this troubling road, we encounter those who care; truly they are — only a phone call away. Because they are near and knowing that God is as close as a prayerful thought, we feel care spread like wings over us, and we can finally sleep.

When I woke up this morning, Lord, my mind filled up with all the unfinished business of my life — indeed, with an accompanying emotional stew of anxiety, panic, dread, and shame. So often the stuff of life seems like too much to handle. But then I turn to you, and I find you are right here with me. You are my reprieve, Lord; you are the best part of every-thing in my world. I call on you, and you calm me. I look to you, and you show me a peaceful way through the chaos. I remember you, and I find a place of rejoicing. Then I realize again that my life in this world is only for a time, but your presence is my eternal reward.

Have no fear for what tomorrow may bring. The same loving God who cares for you today will take care of you tomorrow and every day. God will either shield you from suffering or give you unfailing strength to bear it. Be at peace then, and put aside all anxious thoughts and imaginations. — St. Francis de Sales

*Y*our nearness, dear Lord, is a fact not based on my feelings nor on my circumstances. It is a powerful reality — a goodness that is strong and constant, a place of refuge and stability in this crazy, ever-changing world. I see others struggling without you sometimes, and I just want to tell them that you are here for them. I want to tell them that you have been my source of strength, courage, help, support, and comfort — in fact, everything I need! Please give me the right words to convey, in ways that people can perceive and consider, the reality of your nearness, as well as the blessing of your presence.

> *It is good for me to draw near to God: I have put my trust in the Lord God, that I may declare all thy works.* — Psalm 73:28

*D*ear Jesus, the prophet Isaiah was inspired to call you "Wonderful Counselor." If I paid all of my income to the best human counselor, I would probably be helped on some level, but your love, your Spirit, and your Word have more power to transform my heart and mind than any therapist on the face of the earth. Each day as I walk along with you, I hear you speaking words of wisdom, direction, healing, and insight to me. You're not just any counselor; you are the Wonderful Counselor, and I'm honored and humbled to have you walking beside me today.

$\mathscr{L}$ord Jesus, when I think about "the valley of the shadow of death," I see how it can apply, not only to literal dying but also to life in this world. Compared to heaven, this is a dark valley where shades of sin and death loom and linger. But even in the darkness, I'm filled with faith, hope, and love because you are with me. Your implements of encouragement, guidance, and correction — that is, your Word, your Spirit, and your people — are ever-present reminders that you are leading me safely through the dangers and difficulties of this world.

*F*ather in heaven, thank you for the fellowship I enjoy with my friends here on earth. I love going for walks with them; we talk and laugh and enjoy the beauty around us. But you know, Father, my favorite walks are the ones I take just with you. You point out beauty and wildlife I likely would have missed had I been chatting with someone else. You give me encouragement, talk me through my troubling situations, and remind me of how much you love me. I come away from our walks thoroughly refreshed, filled with new hope and joy. Thank you for these special moments and for being beside me at all times.

> *Yea, though I walk through the valley of the shadow of death, I will fear no evil: for thou art with me.*
> — Psalm 23:4

I know that your friend and disciple, the Apostle Peter, once stepped out on a stormy sea in faith, Lord Jesus. As he kept his eyes on you, he walked atop the waves. It wasn't until his focus shifted to the terrors of the raging elements around him that he began to be overcome by them. Today, you know what tumultuous situations are ahead of me. Whether big or small, Lord, help me remember to keep my eyes on you and to be more focused on your presence with me than the circumstances around me. Thank you that, in this sense, walking on water is possible for me, too!

I just want to thank you today, Lord Jesus, that though the love of other people may come and go, your love is perfect, persistent, and faithful. I know this because you reveal it to me every day as you walk beside me, protecting me, providing for me, encouraging me, teaching me, and leading me along the path of life. In your love, I am satisfied.

> *When thou passest through the waters, I will be with thee; and through the rivers, they shall not overflow thee: when thou walkest through the fire, thou shalt not be burned; neither shall the flame kindle upon thee.* — Isaiah 43:2

*H*elp me walk willingly beside you, almighty God, even when, in my estimation, you're doing things all wrong. I know that sounds strange when I say it out loud, but I admit that when I dig my heels in or grumble or accuse you of not caring, I'm really doubting your wisdom and ability to lead me where I need to go. So, Lord, please help me remember that you know things I don't, that you see clearly from the beginning to the end, and that you love me more deeply than I can ever fully perceive. In light of these realities, I will choose to follow you today without fretting.

> *A*nd Jesus came and spake unto them, saying, All power is given unto me in heaven and in earth. And, lo, I am with you always, even unto the end of the world. Amen. — Matthew 28:18, 20

*L*ord Jesus, it's awesome to realize that all authority belongs to you! I want to remember that, because when it feels as if my day, or my life, or the world is spinning out of control, I can be assured that it really isn't. And when it's hard for me to believe or understand this reality, there's the comforting truth that you are walking with me. Thank you for your promise to be with us who belong to you until you bring this world to a conclusion and settle us in our heavenly home.

Our only task is to keep in step with him. He chooses the direction and leads the way. As we walk step by step with him, we soon discover that we have lost the crushing burden of needing to take care of ourselves and get our own way, and we discover that the burden is indeed light. We come into the joyful, simple life of hearing and obeying.

— Richard Foster, *Freedom of Simplicity*

*J*esus, my redeemer, you are the one who takes my brokenness and gives me wholeness in return. You are the one who takes my mistakes and turns them into blessings. You are the one who forgives my sins and fills me with your own righteousness so that I can be in fellowship with you. How can I praise and thank you enough for coming alongside me and transforming my troubled heart into a rejoicing one? I can begin today by taking my place beside you — the place you have made for me by your redemptive love.

Hold my hand, Lord, so I will not be afraid.

> *And* nd I will pray the Father, and he shall give you another Comforter, that he may abide with you for ever. Even the Spirit of truth; whom the world cannot receive, because it seeth him not, neither knoweth him: but ye know him; for he dwelleth with you, and shall be in you.
>
> — John 14:16–17

How grateful I am today for your Holy Spirit, Lord Jesus! He reveals himself to me as my comforter — the one who teaches me, leads me into all truth, and ministers as my intercessor. No wonder that, even though I cannot see you, Jesus, I can sense your nearness to me. By your Spirit, you walk beside me every step of the way. I praise you for the gift of your presence through the ministry of the Holy Spirit.

One of the ways I hear you speak to me along the path of life, Lord Jesus, is through your Word. Sometimes you remind me of a Scripture that was read during a worship service, or a passage I reviewed during a quiet time with you, or maybe a verse I memorized as a child. I find that your Word is a great source of comfort and strength along my path, and the more of it I take in and think about, the more I understand your deep affection for me. Thank you for the way you open up your Word to me. Amen.

How comforting to know that God tends to us as we move through life's extremes! He is here with us in births and deaths and in stillness and activity. We find the courage to live through these present moments and to move into the future, knowing that we cannot wander so far in any direction that he is not already there.

Lord, help me not run ahead today — that is, ahead of your direction and guidance. Help me not lag behind, either, Lord — that is, behind your call to love and forgive and do what is right. Help me remain in the place to which you call me — that place reserved for me beside you. May I be tethered to your side by my willing hand held in your gentle one. I don't want to miss out on one moment of fellowship with you today.

*L*ord God, your Word tells me to keep in step with your Spirit so that I won't gratify the impulses of my human nature that are harmful and destructive to my soul. I admit that sometimes I wade around in my swamp of selfishness when I could be walking lightly and heartily in fellowship with you. I need your forgiveness today for the ways I've ignored you and turned to my own devices. I truly want to walk beside you in the warmth and light of your presence and the peace of your ways. I'm ready to begin again. Help me keep in step with you today and every day. In Jesus' precious name, I pray. Amen.

*H*eavenly Father, I remember some of the epic experiences of my life. Highlights and "low-lights" parade through my memory, but as they do, I realize that they often lose their power over time. The days and weeks and months smooth the novelty, excitement, pain, and pleasure until I'm engulfed again by "everydayness." I live, and life continually changes me, but one thing remains the same: the fact that you are with me. Nothing changes that — not mountains, not valleys, nor the days that wear them into plains. Thank you, dear Father, for always being you and for always loving me.

$\mathcal{I}$t's good to know, Lord, that whether I speak these prayers aloud or lift them up in silence from the depths of my heart, you hear, you listen, and you respond. I know that sometimes I've complained that you're not answering my prayers. I'm sorry for those times of faithless frustration. I know that you always answer but often not in the timing or the way I expect. I'm glad, though, that you're not bound to my expectations. I've seen you bring wonderful answers to my needs and dilemmas that I never could have dreamed up. Your creativity and perfect wisdom never stop astounding me. I will keep praying to you as long as I live because I know you walk with me.

> *Incline your ear, and come unto me: hear, and your soul shall live; and I will make an everlasting covenant with you.* — Isaiah 55:3

You have often called to me in different ways, Lord, inviting me to walk with you and to experience the blessing of your nearness. Thank you for your kind intentions toward me. I realize now that even when it has taken hardship and struggle to get my attention, your desire has always been to bless me. I'm truly glad you have directed me away from destructive choices and paths and have led me into paths that bring life and peace. I owe you everything, and yet you do not take anything from me that I do not choose to give freely. May I always choose to seek you, Lord, to desire your nearness, and to know the blessings of walking beside you.

You need not cry very loud: he is nearer to us than we think.

— Brother Lawrence of the Resurrection

I would rather walk with God in the dark than go alone in the light. — Mary Gardiner Brainard

*W*alking with you is like an unlimited benefits package, Lord! Without any premium to pay, I have your promise to deliver, protect, answer, be with, rescue, and honor me. Oh, and you have thrown in a long life and salvation on top of it all. Who is as blessed as I am? Only those who also know your love and the wonderful benefits of walking in it. Lord Jesus, help each of us hold fast to you as we point others toward you as well.

Chapter 3

The Lord Always Helps Me

My Lord and Savior, how much lighter I feel in heart and in spirit when I cast my burdens and my cares upon you. Your strength can do what mine falls short of. By giving you my concerns, I'm able to get on with my life with a more loving spirit and a more kind and giving heart, just as you would want me to. Thank you, Lord Jesus, for always taking from me my heaviest loads, so I can bring back that spring to my step and smile to my soul.

$\mathcal{A}$lmighty God, I need your help more than ever. I can't seem to find the answers to the problems that keep plaguing my life. I have tried to use my will to make everything right, but I finally realize that I must now surrender my will to yours and let you do your miracles. And so I give my burdens to you, trusting that you will smooth out all the rough edges and calm all the stormy seas in my life. Thank you, God, for your help in my times of need. Amen.

> *Turn your problems over to God, and he will orchestrate the best outcome.*

> *Blessed is the man that trusteth in the Lord, and whose hope the Lord is. For he shall be as a tree planted by the waters, and that spreadeth out her roots by the river, and shall not see when heat cometh, but her leaf shall be green.*
>
> — Jeremiah 17:7–8

Dear Lord, when the last flicker of hope seems to go out in my heart and my spirit is ready to give up, you come to me and show me more mercy and more grace, and I'm renewed in strength. I know that you will never give me more trouble than I can handle and that in those times when I don't believe I can handle more, you will come to me and carry me through the darkest valleys. For this, Lord, I'm forever grateful.

*H*oly God, things are tough lately, and I could use a helping hand from above to get through it all. Show me how to make the right choices and do the right things to make life more joyful. I ask you today in prayer to stand beside me and be my column of strength when I need something strong to lean upon. My faith in you tells me I can always lean on you, God, no matter how bad things seem to me, for I know that you are here ready to intervene on my behalf. Amen.

No matter how deep a rut we dig ourselves into, the arms of God are long enough to lift us up to a newer life, free from struggle. No matter how dark a tunnel we crawl into, the love of God is strong enough to reach in and guide us toward a brighter life, free from fear.

Today, dear Lord, I ask for your mercy and compassion. Today, I ask for your divine love and wisdom. Today, I ask for your guidance and your strength. I ask that you do for me what is out of my control to do and that you show me the way that my own human eyes fail to see: the way to happiness, joy, and love. I surrender to your loving will for my life, for I know that my mind cannot always grasp the bigger picture you have in store for me. Today, Lord, I ask for your help in keeping me on the path you have made for me and me alone. Thank you, Lord.

Great God in heaven, I'm broken and tired, and I don't think I can carry on much longer without help from you. I've tried all I can to make things work, and still I feel miserable and stuck. I pray that today you will work your mysterious ways in my life and show me open doors that I can't see with my own eyes. Please direct me to solutions that my mind simply can't think of right now. I pray for the miracle of your presence, while bringing a new perspective to my eyes, a new hope to my heart, and a new strength to my spirit. Amen.

> *But thou, O Lord, art a shield for me; my glory, and the lifter up of mine head. I cried unto the Lord with my voice, and he heard me out of his holy hill. Selah. I laid me down and slept; I awaked; for the Lord sustained me.*
> — Psalm 3:3–5

Dear God, I'm filled with gratitude for the awesome ways you always seem to be here for me when I need you most. Either with an inspiration that comes to me from out of nowhere, or a call from a friend when I feel utterly alone, or some wonderful new opportunity that appears when I'm about to give up, you are my miracle worker. I'm truly thankful for the good things you bless me with, as well as the challenges that make me stronger and more resilient. I know that whatever you send my way is for my highest good, and I receive it all with open arms. Thank you, God.

Strengthen ye the weak hands, and confirm the feeble knees. Say to them that are of a fearful heart, Be strong, fear not: behold, your God will come with vengeance, even God with a recompence; he will come and save you.
— Isaiah 35:3–4

Lord God, today is a bright new day, filled with new ideas and opportunities. You never fail to come to my aid by giving me new eyes to see the world with each morning, no matter how dark and long the night before might have been. I awaken, and I feel as though something has shifted, and I know that you have somehow come once again into my heart and refilled it with love and forgiveness and courage, just what I needed in order to rise this morning feeling stronger than ever. You never fail me, God, and I thank you for that. I pray I can always make you proud of me in return. Amen.

Then Jonah prayed unto the Lord his God out of the fish's belly, and said, I cried by reason of mine affliction unto the Lord, and he heard me; out of the belly of hell cried I, and thou heardest my voice. — Jonah 2:1–2

My Lord, I pray to you today from the depths of my heart. I feel as if I can't deal with so much of what is happening around me, and I ask that you help share these burdens with me. With your grace and power, I will be able to conquer what I alone can't conquer and what I alone can't understand. Your gentle helping hand can provide me with the divine guidance I seek, when my own mind can't find the way and when my spirit is unsure. I pray to you, dear Lord, to come to my aid today. Amen.

> *Whenever we are uncertain as to our course, we can rely on God to shut each door against us — every door except the right one.*

Father God, I need a sign today to show me the way toward happiness and joy. I need a word, an image, or a person to appear that my heart and my spirit will recognize as a sign sent from you. Help me discern your loving guidance in the daily events of my life and hear your gentle encouragement when those events threaten to derail my peace of mind. Send me a sign or two today, and give me the wisdom to understand them when I see them. Thank you, Father.

Heavenly Father, I have so many questions that I just can't seem to find the answers for. I feel lost and alone and without direction, as if I'm wandering aimlessly through my own life. I pray that you will help me find the answers I seek and the direction my life should take so that I can live my best life possible. Because you see all the things I cannot and because your perspective is much bigger than mine, I will listen for your guidance and follow the direction of your loving will. Amen.

As the dawn of a new year breaks the horizon, dear Father, I know your eternal love for me goes before me. I ask that you would cause me to live courageously in that love, ready to do and say what is right and good and true in all circumstances. And because I have known your faithful love up to this point in my life, I'm fully confident that all will be well as I move forward and am kept in that same love. Thank you for always walking with me and, at critical times in my life, for carrying me on your loving shoulders. I love you, and I pray in the name of my Lord and Savior, Jesus Christ. Amen.

My Lord, why does it sometimes seem as though nothing is going right and every door available to me is closing in my face? Help me see that it is you closing those doors and leaving open only the right one for me. Help me have the faith and the patience to wait for that open door to appear in my life and not be so anxious that I enter the wrong door. Help me trust in your wisdom and surrender to your will, knowing that soon my door will be opened before me.

How could I ever feel alone, dear God, when you have provided me with so many wonderful friends who rarely let me down? I know that these are human angels you have sent into my life to stand beside me through thick and thin. There is no greater blessing than the love of those who care, and you have given me so many people who care and through whom you do your wondrous workings in my life.

*F*ather God, where are you when I need you? Why, of course, you're right here at my side. I come to you today not to ask for something but to thank you for always being here at the exact moment I need you in the flash of an idea or the certainty of a decision, in the sense of which direction to take or a brilliant inspiration. I know that no matter what is going on in my life, I can always count on you to be with me, telling me exactly what I need to hear when I need it. Thank you so much, Father.

> *Ye know in all your hearts and in all your souls, that not one thing hath failed of all the good things which the Lord your God spake concerning you; all are come to pass unto you, and not one thing hath failed thereof. Therefore it shall come to pass, that as all good things are come upon you, which the Lord your God promised you.* — Joshua 23:14–15

Lord, help me understand why the things that happen in my life sometimes have to be exceedingly difficult. I'm tired of the struggle, and I'm exhausted from trying to keep all the balls I'm juggling in the air. I worry they will fall to the ground and my whole life will shatter. Please send me your merciful grace so I can handle my life with more courage, strength, and patience. Your saving grace renews my spirit and even my physical strength so I can take on each struggle as it comes.

Dear God, I don't need a big bolt of lightning to strike me or a loud voice from the heavens to boom down from above telling me what to do. I know that you speak in much gentler, quieter ways. All I ask today is to be aware of your gentle wisdom when you choose to impart it and that I'm not too busy or stressed out to hear your whispers of guidance when they come. I don't need big shows of your love, God. Small ones will do just fine.

For my thoughts are not your thoughts, neither are your ways my ways, saith the Lord. For as the heavens are higher than the earth, so are my ways higher than your ways, and my thoughts than your thoughts. — Isaiah 55:8–9

Our lives are filled with many questions that may never be answered, but that's okay if we let God lead and direct us. We may not understand why certain things happen or why we have to go through difficult situations, but the one thing we can know for sure is that God is always in control.

$\mathcal{I}$t must make you laugh, Lord God, the way I always try to control everything and think I'm in charge. I know that you're in charge and that is best because right now, I have no idea what I'm doing. When I set my human ego aside long enough to feel your presence there beside me, I know that answers are coming and solutions are only an inspiration away. So forgive me for those moments when I think I'm running this ship, and with your love and support, continue to remind me that you and you alone are in charge!

Dear God, please hear my prayer. I ask for nothing big today, just a little extra love sent my way. It seems as though times have been so trying for me lately that I'm on edge and my patience is wearing thin. Please send me just a little bit of extra courage so I can get through this time with my head on straight and my sanity intact. I know that I can always count on you to carry me where my own feet fear to tread. So carry me now just for a little while. Please, Lord!

> *Wherever we may find ourselves,*
> *God is at the helm of our lives.*

*H*ere I am again, heavenly Father. I know that I lean on you a lot, but there are times when even my best and closest friends can't help me the way you can. I consider you my best friend and my constant advisor, and I trust that once again you will intervene in my life when I'm not sure what to do or say. I know that I can surrender and let your thoughts become mine, and your wisdom guide my feet exactly where I need to go. Thank you for always putting up with me, God.

O God, this is a scary time for me, and I could use your spiritual guidance. I am facing choices that I don't know if I'm really prepared to make, and I know that you can see all of the perspectives that I'm blind to in my small existence. Please help me understand the bigger picture, so I can make the wisest decisions possible, decisions based upon love, compassion and empathy. I ask for your guidance in all my decisions, today and every day, both the large and the small. Amen.

We are sometimes faced with choices that are scary, risky, and untried, but we can make wise decisions if we rely on God's spiritual guidance.

Dear Lord, please lift my spirits higher, because right now they are really low. I try to see the blessings in my challenges, and I know in my heart they are there, but my fears and doubts have a hold on me today. Lift me up out of my troubles and help me see them from a much higher place, where the answers that I never even considered are obvious and the wisdom I have no access to is everywhere. Where you are, Lord, is where my happiness is, so lift my spirits today and help me realize that you have my life in your hands.

On wings of angels you carry me, God, when I'm too tired and worn down to walk on my own. Through the valley of darkness you walk ahead, lighting my way so I don't stumble. In the midst of the storm, you calm the seas so that my ship can safely reach the shore up ahead. At the end of a cold night, you bring warmth and comfort to my broken spirit. Thank you, God, for the constant and infinite love you show me, often when I most feel lost, alone, and unloved. That is when I know I will feel those heavenly wings beneath me, carrying me home to you.

> *He's there with you now. Trust Him. And then expectantly anticipate that at the right time and in the way that's most creative to you and all concerned, He will intervene and infuse you with exactly what you need. What an exciting way to live!*
>
> — Lloyd John Ogilvie

> *Truly my soul waiteth upon God: from him cometh my salvation. He only is my rock and my salvation; he is my defence; I shall not be greatly moved.*
> — Psalm 62:1–2

I put my trust in you, dear Lord, to show me the rainbow at the end of a long and dreary storm. I believe in you, Lord, because you never fail to give me what I need even before I know I need it. You may not be visible to me, but your presence is always felt in my heart, where your love and mercy are available to me in infinite supply. I may not always turn to you first, Lord, but eventually when I realize I need your divine help, I always find my way back to the trust and faith I have in you above all.

*D*ear Lord, you said that I can always deliver my burdens to you and that you will take up my concerns. I try to handle my own problems as much as possible, but today I come to you in prayer because I really need your help. I will listen for your inspiration and instruction, and I will do what you would have me do. I just ask you to make those instructions clear to me, so I know the right steps to take. Help me break through the confusion and fear and see your active presence in my life. Thank you, Lord.

My son, let not them depart from thine eyes: keep sound wisdom and discretion, so shall they be life unto thy soul, and grace to thy neck. Then shalt thou walk in thy way safely, and thy foot shall not stumble.
— Proverbs 3:21–23

*A*lmighty God, please take my cares and my problems and give me a heart free and at peace again. Because my worrying is getting me nowhere, I'm turning it all over to you so you can do that wonderful work of peace that you do. I know that you don't want me to struggle, and my struggling usually comes from fear, doubt, and resistance. Therefore, today, I'm giving my struggles to you, God, knowing that the perfect outcome is on its way.

*I*t's dark outside, Lord, but like a bright and blazing torch, you are there to light my way and warm my heart. It is cold outside, Lord, but like a tent you are there to shelter me from the storms and comfort me. It is scary out there, Lord, but with you always working on my behalf, , I know that there truly isn't anything to fear at all. For that I'm grateful, Lord. Amen.

Chapter 4

God Is Truly Faithful

I remember times in the past, Lord, when I did not know whether I could or should rely on you. In my youth there was a sense that I should be able to handle everything on my own, and I felt like a failure when I couldn't. But through the years, my faith has grown, and I now comprehend the truth that calling on you is exactly the right thing to do in all circumstances. My past experiences have taught me to lean fully on you, dear Lord, not worrying about what is ahead today or in the days to come.

It helps to look over my shoulder and see the times when God was a ready companion. I feel secure, knowing that he is always waiting to take my hand into tomorrow.

$\mathcal{R}$emembering how you have worked in my life, heavenly Father, is what makes me so quick to seek you out for strength and encouragement. I run to you like a little child to a loving parent, whether I'm weeping or rejoicing. I just want to share all of my life with you because I trust your unfailing love for me — a love you have shown to me in so many wonderful ways while I have walked with you. You have never failed to support me. And so I do rejoice in you as I seek your presence today! Amen.

*D*ear Lord, I'm often nearest to you when I'm farthest from security in this life. So often you have used the uncertainties in my world to help me become certain of your presence. I remember, Lord Jesus, the times I had nowhere else to turn, and you were there, assuring me and comforting me. And whenever I've trusted you and put my burdens in your care, I've never been more at peace. I long for that closeness with you today.

Glory ye in his holy name: let the heart of them rejoice that seek the Lord. Seek the Lord and his strength, seek his face continually. Remember his marvellous works that he hath done, his wonders, and the judgments of his mouth.

— 1 Chronicles 16.10–12

*S*omewhere in your Word, God, it says that perfect love casts out fear. It's because of you that I know, in at least one sense, what that passage means. Over and over, your love has become evident to me as I've journeyed along with you through thick and thin. And because of your track record of unfailing love, my troubles don't keep me awake anymore. And when I wake up, if these troubles try to encroach on my morning, I remember that your love is with me, and my fears take a backseat to the faith I have in you.

> *Cause me to hear thy lovingkindness in the morning; for in thee do I trust: cause me to know the way wherein I should walk; for I lift up my soul unto thee.* — Psalm 143:8

It's comforting to have you watching over my life, Father in heaven. Whether I'm awake or asleep, I sense the reality of your presence with me and I'm not afraid. You've taught me that I don't need to fear. Your promise to be with me every day, every hour, and every moment of my life has been upheld and confirmed to me countless times: In my darkest times, I've turned to you, and you've been there; in my most exquisite joys, I've delighted in and with you; and all the times in between, I've talked with you, knowing you hear my prayers. You've continually kept your promise to be with me, and I don't even wonder anymore if you're there. I know you are.

> *As I look back and see God's faithfulness, I'm filled with expectation of all that he has in store for me in the future, and my heart overflows with joy.*

Things might be muddled and messy right now in some areas of my life, Lord, but today I simply lift these up to you in faith. The path I've walked with you up to now is marked with many monuments of your restoration and redemption. In each of these seemingly impossible situations along my way, you have worked to bring about help, healing, and wholeness. That's why I refuse to stress out about what's amiss today. I will do what I know is right and leave the rest in your capable hands.

One day, heavenly Father, I will look back on my entire life and see it from your perspective. Meanwhile, help me learn the lessons you have given me along the way. Particularly, when painful ordeals come and I cry out in my distress, help me remember to look up. Then help me listen to your comforting Word, which reminds me that you are with me and that you have a plan and purpose for me even in my pain — a plan and purpose that begins in fellowship with you and ends in rejoicing with you in my eternal home.

Sometimes, God, the pressures that pile up make me think I'm going to snap like a brittle twig. And just when I think I'm going to be over-whelmed, I call out to you in desperation. It's then that I realize I was trying to make things work through my own strength and according to my own way of thinking. As soon as I turn my face toward you, however, I'm made strong in your strength and strong in the assurance of your help, comfort, and protection. My troubles may be too much for me to handle alone, but as you have shown me time and time again, they're never too much to handle when my hand is in yours.

*I*f I could control my future, Lord, I'd make a mess of my life for sure. If I could see my future, I would never be able to "be" in the present or benefit from it. So please help me relax and leave the future in your hands. The past holds enough evidence to assure me that you're able to carry me through what lies ahead. Let my faith prevail right now because of your faithfulness up to now.

Beloved, think it not strange concerning the fiery trial which is to try you, as though some strange thing happened unto you. But rejoice, inasmuch as ye are partakers of Christ's sufferings; that, when his glory shall be revealed, ye may be glad also with exceeding joy. — 1 Peter 4:12–13

Some of the greatest lessons we learn are only after our hearts have suffered. For in times of pain, we receive wisdom, and in times of sorrow, we gain understanding.

Because faithfulness is part of who you are, Father in heaven, you will never be unfaithful to me. What a wonderful reality! There have been times when I was tempted to believe you had failed me, but whenever I've thought that, I've soon come to realize the truth. I usually catch myself now before I start in with any foolish complaints or accusations aimed at you. It's good to be so thoroughly convinced of how faithful you are, because I know how faithful you've always been. Thank you, Father, that even when I've been unfaithful to you, you have never cast me aside. I pray in the name of your most holy Son, Jesus Christ. Amen.

*H*eavenly Father, I have heard people who have walked with you for decades talk about how good you are to them. Seniors who have spent a lifetime trusting in you are a vast reservoir of testimony about your faithfulness to them. I hear from them how you've seen them through hard times and blessed them in both simple and miraculous ways. Listening to them, dear Father, makes me want to be someone who can easily and readily talk about how you've seen me through and filled me up with good things. My life is open to you — open to receive both your care and your faithful guidance all the days of my life.

$\mathcal{I}$ know I can depend on God to see me through each challenge he allows, because he has always provided the grace and strength I need to endure and ultimately triumph.

$\mathcal{M}$y Lord, why do bad things happen to good people? I don't understand your reasons for allowing so much suffering in some lives. It appears to fly in the face of your goodness and justice and threatens to undermine my faith in your all-knowing, all-powerful, and loving nature. But then I look at Christ: In his life, death, and resurrection, you remind me that there is so much more to life than what meets my eye. Grant me an eternal perspective today, Lord, trusting your wisdom and your final say in all things.

$\mathcal{B}$ecause I will publish the name of the Lord: ascribe ye greatness unto our God. He is the Rock, his work is perfect: for all his ways are judgment: a God of truth and without iniquity, just and right is he.
— Deuteronomy 32:3–4

*D*ear Lord, when good things happen in my life, I often chalk them up to coincidence, good fortune, my own savvy, or something else in the moment they occur. Too often, I fail to see your kindnesses to me for what they are: little I-love-you gifts you send to cheer and encourage me, reminding me that you see me and are caring for every detail of my life. Lord, as I look back on my week and even further back through months and years, I see your tender mercies sprinkled generously throughout my days. I just want to say thank you right now and to tell you that I love you too.

As I consider the goals I'd like to reach for in the year ahead, loving God, perhaps the most worthy ones will center around your love — around giving and receiving your love in various ways and in greater measure. If there are things you'd like to see grow and flourish in my life this year, please turn my heart and mind toward what would nurture those things. In all things, God, I pray that I will honor you by loving well and by remaining in your love from moment to moment, day to day, month to month, throughout the year.

I know you are looking forward to the day, Lord, when we will be together face to face. So am I! I can't wait for the time when I will look back on my struggles and sufferings like a new mother looks on her labor pains — as something fading quickly into the background of her experience because of her profound joy at having and holding that tiny new life. But I must wait. Help me endure patiently as I anticipate.

> *Looking back over the road we've traveled, we sometimes see God more clearly than ever.*

How many sunrises have you granted the world, Lord, up to this day? How many raindrops have fallen on how many harvests? How many meals have sustained how many people throughout the history of humanity? How many hearts have been comforted by your love? What does your faithfulness look like, Lord? Ah, indeed, your faithfulness looks like countless instances of your goodness — so many that we are in danger of taking them for granted. Yet, without these "common" blessings, we begin to suffer and doubt you. We don't wonder why when you give them to us, only when we feel their lack. Perhaps, Lord, reflecting on your goodness is the first step out of my illusion of self-sufficiency. Please strengthen my trust in you today by making me grateful for your faithful ways.

> God is dependable, and his never changing nature reminds me that he is in control.

For I reckon that the sufferings of this present time are not worthy to be compared with the glory which shall be revealed in us. — Romans 8:18

How often, dear God, have you sustained my heart with encouragement from your Word? I recall times when I've heard a sermon passage that was just what I needed to hear, or read a calendar with a verse that lifted my spirits, or received a card on which a friend included a Bible quote reminding me of your love, or remembered a Bible verse I learned long ago in a moment of need. Thank you for every instance of blessing in my life that has come to me through your eternal and sacred Word.

I will worship toward thy holy temple, and praise thy name for thy lovingkindness and for thy truth: for thou hast magnified thy word above all thy name. In the day when I cried thou answeredst me, and strengthenedst me with strength in my soul. — Psalm 138:2–3

O holy God, I most often think about your faithfulness in terms of my physical needs. But where would I be if you hadn't come to minister to my spiritual needs? As I look back and see all that you have provided for my spirit, I rejoice! I see the hope that your promises have brought to my heart; the peace that your presence provides me each day; the balm that your forgiveness is when I confess my sin to you; the comfort that your love gives me when insecurities try to rise up; and the assurance of your strength in me when fear threatens to overwhelm me. My spirit has been brought to life, God, and is kept safe in you!

Ships are guided to safe harbor by the aid of a lighthouse, airplane pilots have the control tower, and space travelers have mission control. Nevertheless, at times, even these helps have failed in some way. Meanwhile, Lord Jesus, as you guide me safely to my eternal home, you never fail. I never have to wonder if your light will go out, if your communication system will fail, or if you will fall asleep at the switch. I have experienced your strong but gentle guidance, and I know it is infallible. Even when I have been weak and failing, you have been ever faithful. I rest securely in your care.

God is our unshakable foundation. He is our unbending column of strength and hope when all seems lost. In the darkest hour, he is the beacon of light that guides us to the safety of solid ground.

*A*nd the very God of peace sanctify you wholly; and I pray God your whole spirit and soul and body be preserved blameless unto the coming of our Lord Jesus Christ. Faithful is he that calleth you, who also will do it. — 1 Thessalonians 5:23–24

I wish, Lord Jesus, I could help everyone understand how truly wonderful it is to walk with you. If I could write a screenplay of my life, the theme of the story would be your faithfulness. If I could recreate the drama of my direst times, my most difficult struggles, my deepest uncertainties, and my most painful disappointments, I would show how perfectly and precisely you intervened, provided, comforted, and helped; indeed, I feel as if I could convince the world! But I know that each person must make his or her own way to you and then decide whether to receive you or not. But for those who would desire you, Lord, grant me a voice to testify to your faithful love.

$\mathcal{M}$y future looks bright to me, dear Lord, even when things don't seem to be going my way. But it's not because I have a Pollyanna kind of optimism. No, it's because so many times I've seen you use the most unlikely circumstances — even redeeming my worst blunders — to bring about something surprisingly marvelous. I don't know how you do it; I just know that you do. So today I'm watching and waiting patiently for what you have in store. Thank you for your excellent plan for my life.

$\mathcal{I}$n retrospect, we can see how God uses every life circumstance, disappointment, and joy to reveal his plan for our good. We can truly trust in God's faithfulness.

*A*s I have let go of my own goals for my life to embrace yours, dear Lord, I have enjoyed great adventure and great challenge. Meanwhile, my faith in you has deepened and your peace has become stronger in my heart. I have learned to love you more with each passing year, and I know without a doubt that you have my good in mind. What a difference this journey with you has made in my character! There is no part of my life that has not been touched for the better by the good purposes you have for me.

I admit, Lord God, there have been times in the past when I thought you were tardy in answering my prayers or remiss in the way you answered them or ignoring me altogether. That was because I was impatient and had expectations and preconceived notions I was trying to impose on your plan. How foolish I feel when I think about them now! But I'm also encouraged by the way your faithfulness to and patience with me has brought about growth and change in my thinking and behaving. A mature faith is developing as I walk with you. I praise you for this, dear Lord!

And we know that all things work together for good to them that love God, to them who are the called according to his purpose. — Romans 8:28

Chapter 5

Cherished Child

Dear God, there are times when I feel totally worthless, as if I just don't matter to anyone. I feel as if no matter what I do, it just doesn't make any difference and that my hopes and dreams are simply not meant to ever come true. And so, I ask in prayer for a new faith in your eternal and unceasing love for me. I know that in your eyes, I'm worthy, and I ask that you help me realize that in my heart, even when the world around me makes me feel small. In your eyes, I know that I matter. Thank you, God.

> *By this I know that thou favourest me, because mine enemy doth not triumph over me. And as for me, thou upholdest me in mine integrity, and settest me before thy face for ever.*
> — Psalm 41:11–12

Thank you, Lord, for making me feel as if I'm your precious child. I may fail at times in this world, but I know there is a place beside you just for me in heaven. I may make mistakes and unintentionally hurt people, but I know you forgive me and are always urging me to do better. I may stumble on my path, but I know you will always pick me up because you love me and because you are my God.

*F*ather in heaven, according to your Son Jesus, each of us is a wonderful miracle of life, whom you created for a purpose. Let me understand my purpose so that my life becomes a masterpiece of living out your will in the world. Let my feet walk where you guide me, and let my voice speak the words you wish me to speak. I may often feel small, but in my heart I know you want me to love others as you love me and to be for others the beacon of hope your Son has always been for me.

I have learned to trust your love for me, Lord. That is why I pray. I talk to you about virtually everything that comes my way in life. I look to you for counsel and wisdom, provision and protection. I would be truly lost if I could not come to you at all times, seek your guidance, and cast my cares on you. Thank you for inviting me here to this place of communing with you. Thank you for always having your doors open and your loving heart ready to receive me.

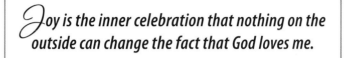

Joy is the inner celebration that nothing on the outside can change the fact that God loves me.

O God, I pray today for those little reminders that you are there for me. I pray for signs big and small that warm my heart and tell me you are watching over me like a loving father, filled with concern and mercy for me. I pray that you will show that same concern and mercy for my family and loved ones. When I sense your love for me, I know that I'm deeply adored and that you will never abandon me in times of need.

> *They that dwell under his shadow shall return; they shall revive as the corn, and grow as the vine: the scent there of shall be as the wine of Lebanon.* — Hosea 14:7

ord, why do I work so hard and strive to be a success at everything? Why do I always feel so empty inside, no matter what I do or achieve? Such a hollow pursuit only serves to make me feel exhausted and uninspired. I wonder for whom it is I'm living my life and to whom I have to prove myself for my sense of worth. Help me know that in your eyes I'm perfect just the way I am. Help me understand that I need not do anything or be someone special for you to love me and cherish me. This I pray, Lord. Amen.

> *No man, when he hath lighted a candle, putteth it in a secret place, neither under a bushel, but on a candlestick, that they which come in may see the light.* — Luke 11:33

God, put me to work and help me realize your grand purpose for my life. I know that as your beloved child, you expect me to be the best I can be and to settle for nothing less. You have created me as a unique expression of your own love, and I long to share that expression with the world. Please empower me with everything I need to go forth and shine this little light of mine — the light you alone have given me to shine.

*L*ord God, I know that I don't have to do anything to earn your love. Just by being born, I know that you thought enough of me to give me precious life and that your love will last even after I'm gone from this world. How good it is to know that there is something in my life that never changes — that is, your love for me! I can depend upon that love and build my life into something that will make you proud to call me your child. In the precious name of Jesus, I pray. Amen.

$\mathcal{I}$ am a priceless masterpiece — a one-of-a-kind, unique treasure whom God loves deeply and eternally. Before I was born, he loved me. He loves me now. And when I am old and gray, he will love me still.

Father God, I thank you for showing me that you love me no matter what happens and no matter how I mess up in life. I strive to do my best and to make you proud and happy, but there are those times when I just don't have enough patience or I act in a way that is inconsiderate or rude. Nevertheless, you still love me! Your acceptance of my flaws as well as my talents is what gives me joy. You love me for who I am and for who I hope to become one day in the light of your care for me. Thank you, Father God.

But I am like a green olive tree in the house of God: I trust in the mercy of God for ever and ever. I will praise thee for ever, because thou hast done it: and I will wait on thy name; for it is good before thy saints.

— Psalm 52:8–9

God's grace is our comfort in times of trouble and our beacon of hope amid the darkness of despair. By opening ourselves to God's ever-present grace, we know we are loved and cared for, and our hearts sing out in joyful gratitude.

Dear heavenly Father, I usually come to you in prayer to ask for help, or for guidance, or for answers to this problem or that. But today, I come to say thank you for the amazing grace you shower upon me. How can I not feel joy in my heart when you make me feel entirely loved and special and cared for? Your presence is a constant reminder that I'm precious and that my life has meaning and purpose. For that I'm truly grateful, because without meaning and purpose, life would be painfully empty. You fill me with love — for myself, for others, but mostly for you, Lord, my beloved Father!

*L*ord God, I sometimes complain and rail against your will in my life, thinking that I know better. But you know me better than I know myself, and you know that even if it hurts me now, your will is the best and highest path to a happy and purposeful future. I often lose patience with your timing, and I want things now, but you have a higher vision for my life that I can only dream of. Please forgive me when I act immaturely and impatiently. I know in my heart that your love for me is steadfast and true. I know I'm your precious child, Lord, even if on occasion I behave like a spoiled brat.

O holy God, I'm in a lot of pain these days, and I feel unloved, lost, and alone. I feel sometimes like an abandoned child, with no one to turn to for comfort and hope. Please help me remember that you promised never to abandon me. Even though I cannot see or hear you, I know in my soul that you are present in my life, even amidst the pain and the chaos. In my narrow-minded human brain, I often focus way too much on what I see with my physical eyes and not enough on what I believe. Help me find my faith **again** and see with a different set of eyes that you love me just as you always have.

> *O Lord, I have heard thy speech, and was afraid: O Lord, revive thy work in the midst of the years, in the midst of the years make known; in wrath remember mercy.*
> — Habakkuk 3:2

Today is a new day, beloved God, and a new opportunity for me to be the person you put me here to be. Today is a new chance to make better choices that reflect your love that is at work within me. It is a new opportunity to let my unique and individual light shine out into the world and serve as a vessel through which your divine love can flow out and touch others. Today is a new day for me to be the best I can be, with your love as my ever-present inspiration and your wisdom as my ever-present guide. Thank you, God, for the gift of this new day and for loving me enough to give it to me.

$\mathcal{A}$s you watch me from above, heavenly Father, there is nothing I need to know except that you are always close by and that your love is always with me. Just to be able to come to you in prayer makes me feel safe and secure as I face the sometimes scary world out there. With you as my loving Father, I know that I'm deeply cherished and that you will never give me anything I can't handle. I walk through my days with this deep sense of peace, and I'm filled with joy and gratitude for your presence.

*W*ho can steal my joy, God, when it is given to me by you? Who can take away my peace? No one, because the joy that comes from being your child and the peace that I have with you by my side is eternal and true. Nothing on earth can shake my faith in you, and nothing can ever make me doubt that I'm cared for by a compassionate and merciful God who never fails to come through for me. Who can make me doubt you are at work in my life, when you have proven to me that you love me in a million ways — both big and small? Thank you, God. Amen.

> *Joy is a celebration of the heart that comes from the depth of my soul. It is the knowledge that my heavenly Father loves me and will always take care of me.*

God is love; and he that dwelleth in love dwelleth in God, and God in him. Herein is our love made perfect, that we may have boldness in the day of judgment: because as he is, so are we in this world.
— 1 John 4:16–17

When you forgive me, Lord God, I know that I'm loved by a God of mercy and compassion and not by a God of wrath and vengeance. You never cease to give me a soft place to fall when life gets a little too hard to handle, and lately that seems to be the case. With undying grace, you act as a caring, doting parent ready to give me advice and aid; yet you also give me the freedom to make my own choices, even my own mistakes. I know that no matter what I do or what I accomplish in my life, the highest achievement of all will be my understanding of just how loving a God you are.

May you know deep in your heart that God is not in love only with what he hopes to make of you in the years ahead; he is in love with what you are right now — a forgiven follower of Jesus Christ.

What is grace but the love of my Savior for me! I sense your grace when I see a child smile at me, reminding me that your love is all around me. I sense your grace when something goes well, knowing that I have purpose in my life. I see your grace everywhere; it is even a part of me! Your loving care never fails, never abandons, and never ends, and I know in every fiber of my being that I shine in your eyes and that is all the grace I need.

Dear Lord, it's been quite some time since I last turned to you for help. I know you are always there for me and that you love me as your precious child, but you know how it is. We like to think we can solve all our problems and make the right choices all by ourselves. I imagine that must make you laugh sometimes. Actually I'm not ashamed to say that I truly need you. I always need you, but today, I really could use some extra loving care and attention to help me overcome the challenges before me. I pray to you, dear Lord, with an expectant and thankful heart.

> *And this is the confidence that we have in him, that, if we ask any thing according to his will, he heareth us. And if we know that he hear us, whatsoever we ask, we know that we have the petitions that we desired of him.* — 1 John 5:14–15

The sun may not come out today, and the people I love may let me down and disappoint me, but, dear God, your love never fails me. The plumbing may not work, my car may go kaput, and my mailbox may be stuffed with bills to pay, but, God, your love never fails me. No matter what I may be dealing with, I'm always able to get back to my center by just remembering that you are my rock and my fortress — my foundation that never shakes or changes from beneath my feet. Thank you, God, so very much.

When the cold has made my body ache, and my legs no longer feel as though they can carry me one more step, I can call to you, my God, to pick me up and carry me for a while. In your loving and comforting arms, I find the peace and rest I need to renew and restore me. In your caring arms, I am healed and strengthened so that you can set me back down upon my path. Thank you, God, for always having those strong and loving arms ready to carry me when I'm too tired and worn down to walk alone.

Always remember: God's love never fails.

> *If thou wouldst seek unto God betimes, and make thy supplication to the Almighty; if thou were pure and upright; surely now he would awake for thee, and make the habitation of thy righteousness prosperous.*
> — Job 8:5–6

Dear Lord, I sometimes feel as though I don't belong, as if I'm on the outside of my life looking in. What is your plan for me? What are your hopes for me? I ask today for your wisdom and guidance so I can live out that plan and realize those hopes. I ask for the strength to keep on moving even when I run into a wall. I ask that you urge me on with love and inspiration when I once again feel unsure of my own footing in life, and I pray that you will show me my rightful place here on earth, as well as your will for me.

As I rise to face another day, God, I'm assured that your love will be there to greet me. I know that throughout this day there will be problems, there will be issues, and there will be drama. But just knowing how much you care for me makes me strong enough to handle anything life has to throw at me and to handle it with grace, dignity, and patience. All the drama in the world cannot shake me when my foundation is your steadfast love for me. Thank you, God.

$\mathcal{I}$t's easy, Lord, to celebrate and be happy when all is going good as gold in my life. But for those times when my life isn't going smoothly, I have to stop and remember that everything happens for a reason and that your love is never gone or diminished. No matter what I have to deal with, you love me more than I can possibly imagine and your love for me never changes, even if I do. Life may be unstable at times, but your love, Lord, is always stable. I pray to you now to say how grateful I am for you, who saw fit to make me your beloved child and give me this amazing blessing called life.

> *$\mathcal{L}$et the people praise thee, O God; let all the people praise thee. Then shall the earth yield her increase; and God, even our own God, shall bless us. God shall bless us; and all the ends of the earth shall fear him.*
>
> — Psalm 67:5–7

*D*ear God, can I turn to you today for help? Can I pray for a sign that you are here, always here, watching over me and protecting me? I feel a little off center and just need to know that you are with me. Knowing that is what keeps me strong and unafraid, and when I lose it, nothing seems right in my world. I know that as I sit here in quiet prayer, I will once again feel that connection. I know it is always here with me, for you never remove your love from me. Help me remember that now.

I cry to the heavens, dear God, in hopes that you will hear my small voice among many, asking for your blessings of love and strength. I am weak and need your courage. I am selfish and need your empathy and mercy. I am confused and uncertain and need your guidance and wisdom. I am alone and need your friendship and understanding. I cry to the heavens in prayer, asking that you turn your face toward me and help me make it through the day with grace and patience. In Jesus' sacred name, I pray. Amen.

Chapter 6

The Lord Will Never Leave Me

Heavenly Father, thank you for always being with me. I'm truly grateful for the promises in your Word, the ministry of your Holy Spirit, and the fellowship of your people. Each of these blessings reveals your presence with me in a powerful way no matter what I may be going through! It's true that my feelings ebb and flow, but you are consistently strong and steadfast. I may not feel you near me at times, but the fact remains that you are with me. Please steady my heart and mind in this truth today.

$\mathcal{D}$ear Lord, money is not the answer to my problems, even when I feel the lack of it. Money goes as quickly as it comes. Even the richest person is in constant danger of "losing it all." But you are the treasure that cannot be lost or stolen. You are the one who has made all things and to whom all things belong. Thank you for my daily needs that keep me tethered to your side, reminding me that I need you and that you are here with me. Today, Lord, I will be content with your provisions, as long as you are with me. How precious is your loving presence!

When I was younger, Lord God, my feelings and circumstances were the gauges I often used to try to discern your demeanor toward me. Today I see how unsound those ways of thinking were. You have told me in your Word what you are like and that you are always with me. The things that are going on around me don't change who you are and what you have promised. Thank you for strengthening my faith so that I can become increasingly aware that you are always walking beside me.

When the winds of change and challenge blow hard into my life, I take refuge in the Lord. Although I can't see him, I know he's always with me, and in that I take comfort and find strength.

> *Let your conversation be without covetousness; and be content with such things as ye have: for he hath said, I will never leave thee, nor forsake thee. So that we may boldly say, The Lord is my helper, and I will not fear what man shall do unto me.*
> — Hebrews 13:5–6

Father in heaven, I know this world is not my destination; rather, it is my faith journey toward eternal life with you. Perfection and healing await me in heaven, but until then, you promise to never leave me. Even in darkness, you will be my light. Even in suffering, you will be my comfort and support. Even in death you will be my peace. And as I go through the ups and downs of my journey here on earth with you, I have my eyes fixed on the goal of heaven, where my faith will become sight, and I will see you clearly and enjoy your presence forever.

If a person firmly believes that God is always with him, then even if he is thrown into the depths of the sea, he will be preserved in body and soul, and will enjoy greater solace and comfort than all this world can offer.

— Julian of Norwich

$\mathcal{M}$y Lord, even when trials and troubles cloud the landscape of my life, obscuring my view of you, let me look out with eyes of faith fixed on your promises so that my circumstances won't cause me to doubt you. I choose to put my trust in you right now, to release my worry about outcomes, and to leave those outcomes with you. I know that whatever happens, you will remain with me and will uphold me with your faithful love.

The Lord also will be a refuge for the oppressed, a refuge in times of trouble. And they that know thy name will put their trust in thee: for thou, Lord, hast not forsaken them that seek thee. — Psalm 9:9–10

The Lord does not leave us to suffer alone. He is with us in our pain, in our sickness, and in our worst moments.

It doesn't matter what is troubling me, Lord, you know what I need, and I can come to you with my hurts and disappointments, as well as my fears and worries. You don't shame or chide me. Thank you for that. You're not the angry, short-tempered God some would make you out to be. Instead, you are a patient and gentle father — strong and fearless, yet tender and attentive. I could not ask for a better leader and companion in life. Even if everyone else abandons me, your presence is more than enough to see me through.

When fears of abandonment haunt me, heavenly Father, please remind me that everything will be all right, because you will never leave me. The truth is that people can be unreliable; they may not always be there for me. Someone may choose to walk away from a relationship with me; friends or family may be forced by circumstances to move away; or death may come to someone I love. Being left behind is painful, Father. It's something I don't know how to handle very well. I need your comfort and the reassurance of your presence with me. By your grace, help me let go of people when I need to, knowing that I can cling tightly to you, the one who will never let me go.

Faith flows when I stop depending on what I think, on what I feel, and on what I see. Instead, I embrace these facts: God loves me. He will never leave me. He wants only the best for me.

*W*here were you, Lord, when I needed you? When I lost my loved one to illness? When I went bankrupt? When I was abused and cheated and powerless? Where were you? It felt as if you were nowhere to be found. It felt as if you had abandoned me. I wondered if you even cared. Where were you? That's how I felt when it was happening. But now, I know the answer. You were with me. I came through it with a new understanding, with a deeper empathy for those who suffer, and with a strengthened faith. I realize now that you were taking care of me, even in those dark times. You never left me, and you never will. Thank you, Lord. Thank you.

The old gospel song "Take My Hand, Precious Lord" expresses my need for you extremely well, Lord God. I understand that it was written during a time of deep sorrow. Please hear it as my prayer today, Lord, as I pour out the troubles in my heart to you. How I need the assurance of your presence with me right now! How I need you to cradle my heart and heal it! Hold me up, I pray, even though I feel as though I will fall and never rise again. Hold my hand securely in yours, Lord. I pray in Jesus' name. Amen.

The steps of a good man are ordered by the Lord: and he delighteth in his way. Though he fall, he shall not be utterly cast down: for the Lord upholdeth him with his hand.
— Psalm 37:23–24

Since you are everywhere at all times, Lord God, there is no way you could ever not be with me. But your Word speaks of a more meaningful way in which you are with me — a personal and intimate fellowship that you bring to my life. It is for this loving way you come alongside me that I praise you today. You are, indeed, the almighty God of the universe, who is all knowing and present everywhere at once and who sees me and has initiated an eternal friendship with me. What a reason to rejoice today, Lord!

*E*ven in lean times, my Creator, you provide for those who walk with you. You are the source of all provision, and to walk with you is to have all I need. Sometimes you have fortified my faith by having me wait on you, and in your timing you have always come through with food, shelter, finances, and clothing when I've been in need of them. Sometimes you have redirected me by withholding what I thought I needed, but that was also part of your provision, a provision of guidance. Thank you for taking such good care of me as I walk with you. You have never forsaken me, not once. What a reason to rejoice today, Lord!

> *No one knows the mind of God, nor why he chooses to work the way he does. But in our most difficult circumstances, we will miss the peace of his presence unless we persevere in trusting that he is always faithful and always good.*

Sometimes I act as if I can boss you around, Lord, but it's foolish of me to think and act that way. Sometimes I get all out of sorts when you don't do things the way I think you should, and I'm sorry for behaving that way toward you. I often need to be reminded that you are sovereign, that you are in charge, and that you know exactly how things will happen. My job is to trust in you, to wait patiently for you, and to find peace in these postures of faith. You are always with me; you are always faithful; and you are always good. I need never doubt you.

$\mathcal{H}$ow peacefully a beloved child or cherished pet sleeps when they know we are near! May I trust your nearness to me in that same way, dear Lord. May I lie down and sleep well, knowing you are here. May I awake and feel safe and secure knowing you go before me into the fray of each day. May I quickly consult your wisdom when difficulties arise. May I stop to praise you when I experience your blessings. May I always be aware of your presence with me and lean into you with trust, love, and gratitude. Amen.

*D*ear Lord, you are the best of friends. I could never find the kind of solace I find in you anywhere else. When I'm troubled and flailing about in my distress, I sometimes flit about from person to person, seeking comfort and help. But then, when I've worn myself out with this anxious activity, there you are, quietly waiting for me, ready to wrap your love and peace around me and take me into the place of comfort and assurance. Thank you for being here for me without fail and for your goodness to me today.

*B*ut the salvation of the righteous is of the Lord: he is their strength in the time of trouble. And the Lord shall help them, and deliver them: he shall deliver them from the wicked, and save them, because they trust in him.

— Psalm 37:39–40

Thank you, heavenly Father, that when I have "ugly days" — when I'm out of sorts and don't even like being in my own skin — you don't turn away from me in disgust. Sometimes I have a hard time believing you are still here with me after the way I've behaved. Every time I come to my senses and turn my heart to seek you in prayer for help and forgiveness, you are with me. And when I come to you, I don't find a toe-tapping, tsk-tsking Father, but rather, one who reminds me of his love for me and who is happy I have come to him to get cleaned up and back on track. I'm blessed to be your child and to have you as my eternal Father.

*M*y Lord, how often human love fails, my own included! Our so-called love is usually made of different stuff than yours is. We often fashion our love gifts for one another like Trojan horses, filled with expectations of something we'll get in return. Sadly, Lord, too many of my love offerings to others are merely a selfish imitation of your selfless, eternal love for me. Please teach me to love as you love, for your love always protects, always hopes, and always perseveres. Truly, it never fails. Thank you for your ever-present, unfailing love.

Rejoice! For God's love never fails.

O God, thou hast taught me from my youth: and hitherto have I declared thy wondrous works. Now also when I am old and greyheaded, O God, forsake me not; until I have shewed thy strength unto this generation, and thy power to every one that is to come.

— Psalm 71:17–18

*W*hen I feel alone, dear Lord, remind me that I'm never alone because you are always with me. When I feel lonely, let me open my heart to your friendship. When I'm rejected, flood my soul with a deep sense of your acceptance. When I fail, let me be quick to seek your comfort and forgiveness. When I'm in awe of your creation, let praise flow from my lips toward you. Whenever, wherever, whatever I may be experiencing in life, Lord, may I instinctively turn toward you to find you with me, ready to engage with me in the moment and being everything that I need and long for.

From youth to old age, Lord God, you remain with those who walk with you. You never take vacations from your children. You never hire a babysitter. You never run out on us or leave us with relatives. You stay with us, not as an obligation, but as one who cherishes and delights in us. What a wonderful thing to consider! I'm not a burden or a hassle to you, Lord; you like being with me. And it's not because of anything special I do; it's because you are so thoroughly good and kind, tenderhearted and merciful toward your children. How wonderful you are! How wonderful it is to walk with you my whole life through!

Under his wings I am safely abiding, though the night deepens and tempests are wild; still I can trust him, I know he will keep me, he has redeemed me and I am his child. — William O. Cushing

Almighty God, someone has said that we should never doubt in the darkness what you have shown us in the light. But the intensity of darkness sometimes causes me to forget what I've seen in the light. Truly, I could never navigate this darkness without you here with me to remind me of what is true! I could never venture out into the unknown if I did not know you were with me — you, the all-knowing one! And if I look at anything or anyone but you as the uncertainty of the future looms ahead, I quickly lose heart. But as I keep my eyes on you, my hand in yours, I confidently go forward.

The Lord gives me the faith to take the next step, even when I don't know what lies ahead. He gives me the assurance that even if my faith falters, he will never abandon me.

Comfort comes to God's people in their times of need.

*I*t has taken some time for me to understand that you will never leave me, Lord. I tend to project onto you my own tendencies or the things I have experienced at the hands of others. Please forgive me for thinking of you in these terms. You don't deserve my doubt and suspicion, but you have patiently endured my fears and misplaced accusations until I have understood the truth about your faithful love for me. Thank you for not giving up, for being kind when I was not, and for being gentle when I was angry and quick to judge your timing and ways. I was slow to learn, but now I place trust in the certainty that you are with me and will never fail me.

*B*less you, Lord God! Bless you for your goodness to your children! Bless you for never leaving or forsaking us! Bless you for loving us without our having to earn your love! My heart is full of thanks and praise because you are with me. My soul has a deep and abiding security because you will never leave me. My spirit rejoices because you have brought me near to you through your great salvation. I am richly blessed. Receive my praise, dear Father! May such praise bless your heart today.

Thank you, Lord, for your grace, love, and fellowship. Thank you for all the ways you minister to all my needs — spiritual, emotional, and social. Today, when I sense my need for grace, I will turn to you and find you here. When I need love, here you will be ready to assure me of your own. When I need fellowship and friendship, here your Spirit will be ministering and communing with me. How grateful I am that I am never without what my heart and soul need because you are always with me! Amen.

Chapter 7

God Carries Me Through Trials

Lord God, I often wonder why we have to struggle so much and feel so much pain in life. In my case, I know it must be for my own good, but I do wish it would end soon. And since I find it hard to deal with it on my own, I come to you in prayer today to ask for your help. With your strength, I know I can handle this present pain, knowing that this, too, shall pass. I just don't think I can do it alone, Lord. Please let me lean on you today.

It seems really dark outside, God, even though the sun is shining and the sky is clear. I have a lot on my mind and so many things to think about. I'm also feeling lost and alone without a friend in the world. I need someone stronger than I am to carry me through these trials, and I know that your loving arms provide just the right comfort and strength to make me feel as though I can do anything. God, walk with me today, just in case my feet fail me. I know you will be there to catch me when I fall. Thank you, God.

> *In the midst of our troubles, God comes to us. In the darkness, his Spirit moves, spreading light like a shower of stars breaking through a stormy night sky.*

$\mathcal{I}$ pray to you today, heavenly Father, to thank you for the constant and reassuring presence you have become in my life. I remember a time when I tried really hard to go it alone, and wow, what a mess I made of things! But knowing that you are always beside me, during bad times and good, helps me feel secure even in the most insecure of situations. I cannot tell you what a difference that has made in my life, but then, I imagine you know my own soul. Thank you, Father.

My strength and my weakness are in the Lord's hands. He preserves my strength and helps my weakness. Where the door is shut, he will open at my knocking.

*D*ear God, I have heard people say when one door closes, another door opens in its place. Today I ask in prayer that I may see that new opportunity for happiness open up to me. I have knocked, and my heart is now tired and hurt, and I'm in need of a new hope to carry on. Please be the strength that I do not have, and please provide me with the faith I struggle to believe in when all doors around me seem to be closed. I know that you will open one, and I ask in prayer that it be soon. Amen.

I'm thankful, Lord, that when I'm too weak, you give me strength and, when I'm too tired, you infuse me with new energy. I'm thankful that when I'm too frightened, you give me courage to move forward in the face of fear. I'm thankful that when I'm confused, you show me a clear vision and a direction with purpose. For so many things I'm thankful, Lord, because when I'm facing the impossible, your presence makes all things possible.

As for me, I would seek God, and to God I would commit my cause. He does great things and unsearchable, marvelous things without number. He gives rain on the earth and sends waters on the fields; he sets on high those who are lowly, and those who mourn are lifted to safety.

— Job 5:8–11

Dear Father in heaven, as your faithful child, I know that I can turn to you for the courage I lack when I'm in need of it. I pray today for a little extra courage and perhaps even a bit of patience. I'm being challenged and don't want to lose my cool and react in anger, because when I do there is never anything good that can come from it. Please help me keep my temper in check, my tongue in place, and my heart calm as I deal with my challenges today. With your help, I know I can make things right again.

> *Whom have I in heaven but thee? and there is none upon earth that I desire beside thee. My flesh and my heart faileth: but God is the strength of my heart, and my portion for ever.* — Psalm 73:25–26

I do not fear the dark, Lord, when I know that I have you as my shining light to guide me. I do not shudder from the cold, Lord, when I feel your constant presence warming me. I do not back down from challenges, Lord, when I sense you standing beside me, ready to offer me your strength and fortitude. Nothing can shake my faith in you, for you are my rock, my fortress, and my comforting balm in times of trouble. You are my light, my guide, and my director in this play called my life. Thank you, Lord.

*S*ometimes emotional or psychological pain can burn so deep within me that it scorches the center of my soul, bringing me utter darkness and despair. Yet even in this most terrible pain, I can turn to the Lord for courage, comfort, strength, and the victory he lovingly offers me, while giving me light and hope to see me through.

*W*hen the weight of my despair threatens to pull me under, I know that you, Lord, will take me by the hand and pull me out of the deep waters and place me upon dry land. No matter how much I cry and hurt, I feel a place deep within where you reside, and I know that these painful times will pass and that I will heal with time and patience and your love. I would rather not go through this pain, but I do so with confidence and faith that it is for my spiritual growth and that I will come out the other side a stronger and better person. Amen.

O God, I'm truly grateful to have you as my rock to stand upon and my soft place to fall should I stumble along the way. You provide me with strength when I need it and gentle loving care when I need that, too. There is nothing here on earth that can fill the emptiness inside me but you, O God. I'm always whole and always at peace because of your love for me, and for that I am truly grateful.

For which cause we faint not; but though our outward man perish, yet the inward man is renewed day by day. For our light affliction, which is but for a moment, worketh for us a far more exceeding and eternal weight of glory.
— 2 Corinthians 4:16–17

> *God meets us in our weakness and turns our weakness into strength.*

Dear heavenly Father, just as you have been a source of strength for me, please become that source for my family and friends. So many of my loved ones seem to be going through such awful challenges lately, and I don't always know the best way to help them. Guide me to say and do just the right things to help them feel stronger and more capable so that they can rise up and meet their problems with newfound faith and fortitude. Just as you are a light in my life, Father, let me now be that light for others wherever and whenever I can. I pray in Jesus' name. Amen.

My Lord, let me lean on you for a while. I have little strength left right now and my hopes have faded. Let me find some comfort in your love and your guidance. I will surrender my thoughts and my will to you, and I will stop trying to fix everything. I will let you guide me to the right way to repair all that is broken in my life. Let me rest with you awhile. I'm tired and want a little peace in my life right now. I don't ask that you lift these difficulties from my life, only that you help me get through them.

Come, and let us return unto the Lord: for he hath torn, and he will heal us; he hath smitten, and he will bind us up. After two days will he revive us: in the third day he will raise us up, and we shall live in his sight.

— Hosea 6:1–2

Holy God, you have chosen to bless me with so many material things, but today I want to thank you for those immaterial things that mean even more to me. You have blessed me with faith and hope in things unseen. You have blessed me with love for my family, for my friends, and for the world. You have blessed me with strength, patience, and tolerance when dealing with others. You have blessed me with a sense of humor and humility. I could go on and on listing the blessings you've bestowed upon me. For now, let me just say thank you, thank you, thank you!

*W*hen the hard rains fall, dear Lord, you are like the umbrella that shields me from the cold and the harshness of the storm. You are the sun that comes out afterward to warm my heart again and bring life to all that was dead inside me. I know that suffering is a part of life, but I don't have to like it. I do accept it, though, knowing that it is helping me grow and become stronger and more resilient. Please keep that umbrella handy, dear Lord. I never know when I might need you. Yes, I do know — I always need you.

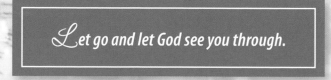

Let go and let God see you through.

If we would stop pretending to be strong, start being honest with ourselves and God, and cry out, "God, please help! I am poor and needy," he would hurry to help us and be our strength.

Dear God, how you must laugh when we pretend that we are so strong and brave, and yet inside we are shaking and trembling like a frightened animal! But instead, you show us mercy and grace by supplying us with the strength and courage we lack so that we can stand tall against any enemy — real or imagined. How we must seem so silly to you with our petty problems! But instead, you show us love and compassion and make us feel loved, cared for, and protected. Thank you, God.

If thou wilt walk in my ways, and if thou wilt keep my charge, then thou shalt also judge my house, and shalt also keep my courts, and I will give thee places to walk among these that stand by. — Zechariah 3:7

$\mathcal{L}$oving Father above, do my problems seem petty from your perspective? To me they're big and scary, like demons I struggle with daily. Help me find the higher vision so that I can see the bigger picture you see. I ask for your strength where mine comes up short and for your wisdom where mine is sadly inadequate. I know in my heart that you have planned a purposeful life for me. Just help me see that higher purpose so I can move beyond the day-to-day problems with courage, faith, and hope for tomorrow.

I find it really hard to just let go and surrender my problems to you, my heavenly Creator. I know you can handle them far better than I can, but I guess the control freak in me is really strong. Please help me learn how to let it all go and to trust in your ability to handle the things I just can't seem to get a grip on lately. Please, Lord, strengthen my faith and give me the courage to put my problems squarely where they belong — in your loving and caring hands.

*T*hank you, thank you, and thank you, God, for doing for me what I can't do for myself. It seems that each and every time when I say to myself, "How can I get through this?" you provide me with the courage, strength, and determination I need, not to mention your guidance and direction. Your love and attention never fail me, even when my family and friends are not here for me. I know that I can depend upon you and you alone to never let me down, and for that I'm more and more grateful each day. People in my life may come and go, but you, God, are my rock and my hope forever. Amen.

Then the eyes of the blind shall be opened, and the ears of the deaf shall be unstopped. Then shall the lame man leap as an hart, and the tongue of the dumb sing: for in the wilderness shall waters break out, and streams in the desert.

— Isaiah 35:5–6

My Lord, I usually ask you for things that are material — things like more money to pay the bills, nicer clothes to wear, a bigger house in which to live, and a more reliable car to drive. But, in truth, I know that the greatest gifts you give me are worth far more than all of those things put together. I can survive with little if I know that you are in my world, for you are a constant, loving presence that I can turn to and walk with at anytime. Your strength and love are what make life worth living, not all those other things. With you in my life, I know that I will live, and live abundantly, in all the ways that really matter.

Daniel answered and said, Blessed be the name of God for ever and ever, for wisdom and might are his. And he changeth the times and the seasons: he removeth kings, and setteth up kings: he giveth wisdom unto the wise, and knowledge to them that know understanding. — Daniel 2:20–21

Father in heaven, I pray to you today for help and hope, both of which are in short supply in my life. I need help moving beyond the drama and issues I can't seem to ever resolve, and I need the hope to believe there is a light at the end of this long, dark tunnel. You have helped me through so many trying times that I know you won't let me down, but hurry with that help and hope soon. I'm at the end of my rope and need your love to hang onto.

Dear Lord, you are my nightlight when I'm afraid of the dark. You are my comforting blanket when I'm cold and shivering. I thank you for all that you are to me. I thank you most of all for the peace I have in knowing that no matter what goes on, you are here to lead me through it. I have nothing to fear with you as my loving Father, and everything to believe in and hope for. Thank you, Lord.

In the midst of the darkness that threatens to overwhelm us lies a pinpoint of light — a persistent flicker that guides us through the pain and fear, through the hopelessness and despair, to a place of peace and healing on the other side. This is God's Spirit, leading us back home like the lighthouse beacon that directs the ships through the fog to the safety of the harbor.

Dear heavenly Father, I'm your child — your beloved child here on earth. Please work through me, so I can help others as you have helped me. I want to be like you in every way, using your strength and your wisdom to work miracles in other people's lives, even as you continue to work miracles in my life. I also want to be your faithful child, so you can be a light in the world through me. I pray in Jesus' holy name. Amen.

God, I follow your light as I walk through my dark valleys. Sometimes your light seems so dim that you appear far away, and so I rest in my faith knowing that if I keep moving in the right direction, you will be there to meet me halfway. I ask in prayer that you continue to show me the way to peace and joy and to be the strength that I often can't find within myself. I do see your light, dear God, calling me forward. And faithfully I will follow you wherever you take me.

Father, who but you is my fortress and my strength? I can lean on my loved ones for only so long, but they have fears and problems of their own. You, though, never deny me the love and care I seek. You never turn away from me in times of need or despair, no matter how angry and impatient I become. What a blessing it is to know that I can always count on you to be there when no one around me can be counted on! Thank you for your steadfast presence and faithfulness to me.

$\mathcal{M}$y lips shall greatly rejoice when I sing unto thee; and my soul, which thou hast redeemed. My tongue also shall talk of thy righteousness all the day long: for they are confounded, for they are brought unto shame, that seek my hurt.

— Psalm 71:23–24

Lord God, I sing out today to tell the world that you are the rock upon which my feet hold fast and the fortress behind which I'm safe from all the storms and battles of life. I sing out today to tell the world about your undying love for me, your work in me, and the blessings you shower upon me each time I come to you as your beloved child. Hear my song of happiness and gratitude, God, for I sing out today to thank you for everything you have done for me.

> Then Jesus said unto them, Yet a little while is the light with you. Walk while ye have the light, lest darkness come upon you: for he that walketh in darkness knoweth not whither he goeth. While ye have light, believe in the light, that ye may be the children of light.
> — John 12:35–36

Chapter 8

Pray Even in the Midst of Doubts

Heavenly Father, you have taught me that you would rather hear a tirade of honest frustration from me than a litany of false devotion. As one psalmist wrote, you are the God who desires "truth in the inward parts." So, Lord, help me as I work through my thoughts of feeling let down by you. When things don't go the way I want, I sometimes feel as if you aren't here for me. So I'll pour my disappointments in prayer, knowing that you already know all about my doubts but also that you invite me to come to you and tell you what's in my heart.

You may be working out another plan, Lord God, but I can't see that at this moment. In fact, it feels as if everything that can go wrong has gone wrong. I can't fathom what you're doing. Why don't you help me? How long do I have to wait until I get some relief? Are you even listening to me? I believe you are, but your silence baffles me. I know that you're not indifferent, but that's what it feels like while I desperately need your help. My faith needs a lift, so I'm asking you once again, Lord. Please help me. Please help my unbelief!

Even when we falsely blame God for our disappointments, he is always ready to listen to our complaints. How great is his mercy and love toward us!

Righteous art thou, O Lord, when I plead with thee: yet let me talk with thee of thy judgments: Wherefore doth the way of the wicked prosper? wherefore are all they happy that deal very treacherously? — Jeremiah 12:1

$\mathcal{M}$aybe my disappointment is a small thing in the scope of eternity, but it's a big thing to me right now, Lord. I had hoped for a different outcome, but it just didn't happen that way. I had prayed for your intervention, but it didn't come — at least, not in the way I had hoped. I had wanted things to turn out for the best, but now everything seems to have fallen apart. I don't want to feel anger toward you, but I do right now. I believe it will pass and you will help me find perspective on all of this, but until then, I need your grace and mercy to help me move toward that place of acceptance, trust, and peace.

God answers our prayers in his own way. If his answers disappoint you, remember that he often uses adversity to reveal that he is our refuge and strength, a very present help in trouble.

I thought that following you, God, would make my life far easier, but I see that's not really the case. In fact, this process of building my faith is downright painful at times. Sometimes I wish I could just stop and go with the flow, take the path of least resistance, and forget this narrow road that leads to life. But I don't really want to abandon the path and stop following you. Please help me though these growing pains. I really need your grace and strength. Thank you, God, for being with me and for nurturing me.

My soul is weary of my life; I will leave my complaint upon myself; I will speak in the bitterness of my soul. I will say unto God, Do not condemn me; shew me wherefore thou contendest with me.

— Job 10:1–2

$\mathcal{S}$ometimes, Lord, it feels as though you're against me instead of for me. I know your Word says, "If God is for us, who can be against us?" But when it seems as though your hand is against me, what am I to make of it? It's miserable, and I just want you to leave me alone and stop bringing so much hardship my way. I know you could stop it. Why don't you? Are you angry with me? Is there sin you are trying to point out to me? What do I need to do to cause you to quit heaping troubles on me? O God, please come and comfort me. Show me what you mean by all of these hardships. I long to understand what's going on, and I long to feel that you are, indeed, still "for me."

hank you, Lord, for not rejecting my prayers to you when they are full of frustration and weariness. I don't want to be a chronic complainer, treating you like the Complaint Department, but I do want to talk to you about what concerns me today. I will lay out my troubles before you and put them into your hands. Please renew my heart, soul, mind, and strength even now so that, despite my trials, I will truly live full of my love for you.

I cried unto the Lord with my voice; with my voice unto the Lord did I make my supplication. I poured out my complaint before him; I shewed before him my trouble. When my spirit was overwhelmed within me, then thou knewest my path. — Psalm 142:1–3

Persistent prayer is the greatest act of faith.

*W*hy, Lord, when I have tried to be good to others and do right by them, do they return evil for my kindness? Backstabbing, betrayal, slander, rejection, any and all of it is deeply hurtful to me. I care about others. I really do. I don't wish any ill on them. Meanwhile, I detest mocking and mean-spiritedness. And yet I find these arrows flying my way from people I have tried hard to love in the way you would have me do. I'm smarting from these wounds, Lord. Please help me heal and help me not to become bitter, even though I feel so angry. Renew my love, I pray.

Heavenly Father, I don't know why you continue to withhold the deepest desire of my heart. You must have a reason, but all I know is that I keep longing, and you keep saying no. It feels as if you're rejecting me when I see others around me getting the things they want, and especially when you grant them the very thing for which I've been asking. It hurts deeply, and I don't know how to understand it. Help me trust your wisdom, your plan, and most importantly, your love for me.

> *When we expect God to respond to our problems exactly as we desire, we will frequently be disappointed. More often than not, God does not think the way we think.*

Oppressive people, difficult situations, and unwanted thoughts eclipse my peace and joy, Lord. I feel cornered and trapped when these things rise up against me. I'm not equal to them in my own strength. I feel defeated and depressed when they come marching out to meet me. Please fight for me, Lord! Train me to stand up with you in truth and love and to send these enemies of my soul packing. I can be joyful and peaceful when I fully entrust myself to you.

> *The Lord also will be a refuge for the oppressed, a refuge in times of trouble. And they that know thy name will put their trust in thee: for thou, Lord, hast not forsaken them that seek thee.* — Psalm 9:9–10

I've heard it said that we should be thankful that you don't give us everything we ask for, Father. I can look back and see that that's true when I consider some of the things you've withheld from me when I thought I knew what would be best for me. Some reasons for your "no" answers aren't so apparent, though. It's harder to give thanks for those times, but I will thank you anyway today for keeping me from unseen disasters, miseries, and regrets. And I'll trust you, even though I feel disappointed and saddened when your answer to my desperate pleas are met with a wisdom beyond my own that lovingly but firmly says, "No, child.".

Dear Lord God, when I'm struggling, your "no" responses are not nearly as difficult to accept as your silence. What does it mean when you leave me waiting in the deafening stillness after I have poured out my heart to you? Where are you when I need to feel you near, but it seems you are really far off somewhere? I would rather hear you say anything to me, even if it's something that will be painful to hear than to have you answer me with a stone wall of silence. Perhaps it is not that you are being silent. Maybe I'm just not tuned in to hear what you are saying. In any case, please grant me the understanding to know what I need to perceive.

*I*n my prayers, I have brought my praises to you, along with my requests, confessions, and complaints, Lord. You have always welcomed me into your presence to tell you what is on my heart and mind. Thank you for having an open door for your children to come to you with their bundles of thoughts, feelings, concerns, and needs. I don't know what I would do without your invitation to boldly come into your throne room of grace — to find grace and mercy in time of need. Help me avail myself of your invitation! I pray in Jesus' name. Amen.

Oh that I knew where I might find him! that I might come even to his seat! I would order my cause before him, and fill my mouth with arguments. I would know the words which he would answer me, and understand what he would say unto me.
— Job 23:3–5

I think that the presence of evil and suffering in the world is the hardest thing to understand about life and about your permissive will, Lord. People sometimes ask me, when I tell them that I trust in you, "How can a loving God allow children to suffer?" What shall I say, Lord? You do allow it. I know you do not desire it and that it's our own departure from your good ways that invites and creates suffering. And one day you will do away with all suffering and evil, but until that time, Lord, we coexist with it, and it's hard to perceive why you allow it. Help me be your hands and feet, your heart and voice to those who suffer so that they can understand that your perfect will is for healing and wholeness and for life and love.

> *If we believe that God causes our suffering, we need to turn to the Bible to learn that God is our creator, savior, healer, and protector.*

$\mathcal{I}$ can see how, over time, my disappointments have helped bring me a more mature perspective, Lord. It makes perfect sense when I look at parent-child relationships here on earth. Children who are indulged, given everything they want, and are pampered and coddled are naturally self-centered. Their perspective has never been broadened to take in the considerations of others. What a tragedy it would be if you treated your own children that way! So thank you for the adversity and disappointment that has come my way from your hand. I have learned to trust you and love others in ways I would not otherwise have known.

$\mathcal{W}$e are troubled on every side, yet not distressed; we are perplexed, but not in despair; persecuted, but not forsaken; cast down, but not destroyed.

— 2 Corinthians 4:8–9

> *I prayed but received no answer; I believed but nothing changed; I waited and grew anxious. And so, I went to God to help my failing faith!*

Heavenly Father, losing loved ones is agonizing. I know death is not final and that you have promised resurrection for all and eternal life for those who love you. But this life is where I still am, and saying goodbye is sometimes crushing. The grief engulfs and overwhelms me, and only time can heal it. But time moves slowly when grief is with me. I wish death didn't have to come and steal away the people I love. But it does, and one day it will steal me away. O God! Please be my comfort and my steady hope. I trust in you. Amen.

In the wee hours, Lord, when I can't sleep because my heart and mind are troubled, you hear my prayers. I keep asking you to help me, to give me wisdom and insight, to provide and protect, and to rescue me and restore peace. I pray because I cannot help it. Who else should I ask for help? Who else is able to intervene for me? Only you. And then in the stark reality of daytime, the issues about which I called out to you are still before me. I wonder how and when you will respond. I wait and wonder. O Lord, please don't make me wait forever!

> *But unto thee have I cried, O Lord; and in the morning shall my prayer prevent thee. Lord, why castest thou off my soul? why hidest thou thy face from me?* — Psalm 88:13–14

Dear Father, why do natural disasters happen in the world? Earthquakes, floods, famine, hurricanes, and disease plague our world and wreak havoc on humanity. What purpose can these disasters possibly serve? Isn't it enough that we suffer from the normal strife of living and dying? Must these horrific disasters swallow people's lives, and especially the lives of babies and little children? But then I see your compassion flow from those who come to help and heal when these disasters strike. I hear that people are sometimes better off than they were before after the relief flows in from around the world. I don't understand all your ways, but I see you at work in the world, transforming tragedy into a sort of saving grace. Show me how I can cooperate with you in this — to bring your love and compassion to those who are suffering today.

*Y*ou're a convenient target for blame, Lord, when things don't go right. It happens more than I want to admit that I turn an accusing look your way when I'm not happy with how things are shaping up. I think, Why did you let this happen? or Why didn't you do it this way? or What am I supposed to do now that you've wrecked my plan? If only I praised you for all of my blessings as much as I chide you for all of my frustrations! Help me, Lord, to blame you less and praise you more.

> *When we fail to trust God, we blame him for our struggles. So believe in him, and never lose faith in the Lord.*

Trouble will come to me in this world; you've told me this in your Word, Lord. But it can still sometimes take me by surprise and make me lose sleep when I have to deal with unexpected trouble in my life. You've said I need not worry because you have overcome the world, but it's difficult not to worry when I'm feeling overcome by the world. Troublesome people and circumstances are stealing my joy. Please help me rest in you today, Lord. I pray in your name. Amen.

> *Hath God forgotten to be gracious? hath he in anger shut up his tender mercies?*
>
> — Psalm 77:9

How am I supposed to love these unlovely people in my life, Lord? They can make my day go south faster than any other problem I face. I hate it when my day is going well and one of them comes and turns everything sour with a terrible attitude and discouraging words. I just want to run when I see such people coming. If only I could! Please show me how to shake off the residue of these encounters and resume a spirit of peace and joy. Help me remember to pray for these people. They need your love too.

We prayed but didn't feel answered. Looking back now, however, we realize God did answer but in his own profound way.

When my soul is parched, O God, when my prayers seem as if they're simply echoing into empty space, revive my spirit with your Word. Uplift me by helping me to hope again in your promises. Remind me of your perfect track record of faithfulness so that I won't lose heart and stop lifting my voice to you. If you didn't encourage me during those times, almighty God, I think I would lapse into despair, but your Word is always within reach, and your Spirit is always here to help me understand and believe what is written in your Word.

Hear my prayer, O Lord, and let my cry come unto thee. Hide not thy face from me in the day when I am in trouble; incline thine ear unto me: in the day when I call answer me speedily.

— Psalm 102:1–2

When I pleaded with you, Lord, for that thing I believed would make me truly happy, and you didn't comply, remember how angry I was? I was really mad at you! But you held your ground. It was when I perceived how destructive that thing would have been in my life that I knew you loved me and would rather have me angry for a season than hurt for a lifetime. Thank you for loving me so much.

> *As for me, I will call upon God; and the Lord shall save me. Evening, and morning, and at noon, will I pray, and cry aloud: and he shall hear my voice.* — Psalm 55:16–17

Though my valleys may be deep and long, Lord, yet you are here with me. When the path before me is steep and treacherous, please help me remember that you will strengthen me and keep me safe. The sun may not shine for many days on end, but remind me that you are my light and my salvation. The rain may fall and the wind may blow, but if you tell me that you are my shelter and my comfort, I will not be dismayed. Though I encounter many trials and troubles along the way, Lord, you are truly my everything, and I will put my trust in you. In Jesus' sacred name, I pray. Amen.

Chapter 9

The Lord Understands Our Suffering

Dear Lord, who can relate to my suffering better than you can? That's why I come to you in prayer — because I know that you understand what I'm going through and because you know the higher purpose my suffering serves. I know that I can't see the light that exists at the end of this long, dark tunnel. But I also know that the light is there and that you are with me as I move closer to it each day. You know my pain, and you know why I must experience it. I have faith, Lord, that all will be well and right in my world soon. Amen.

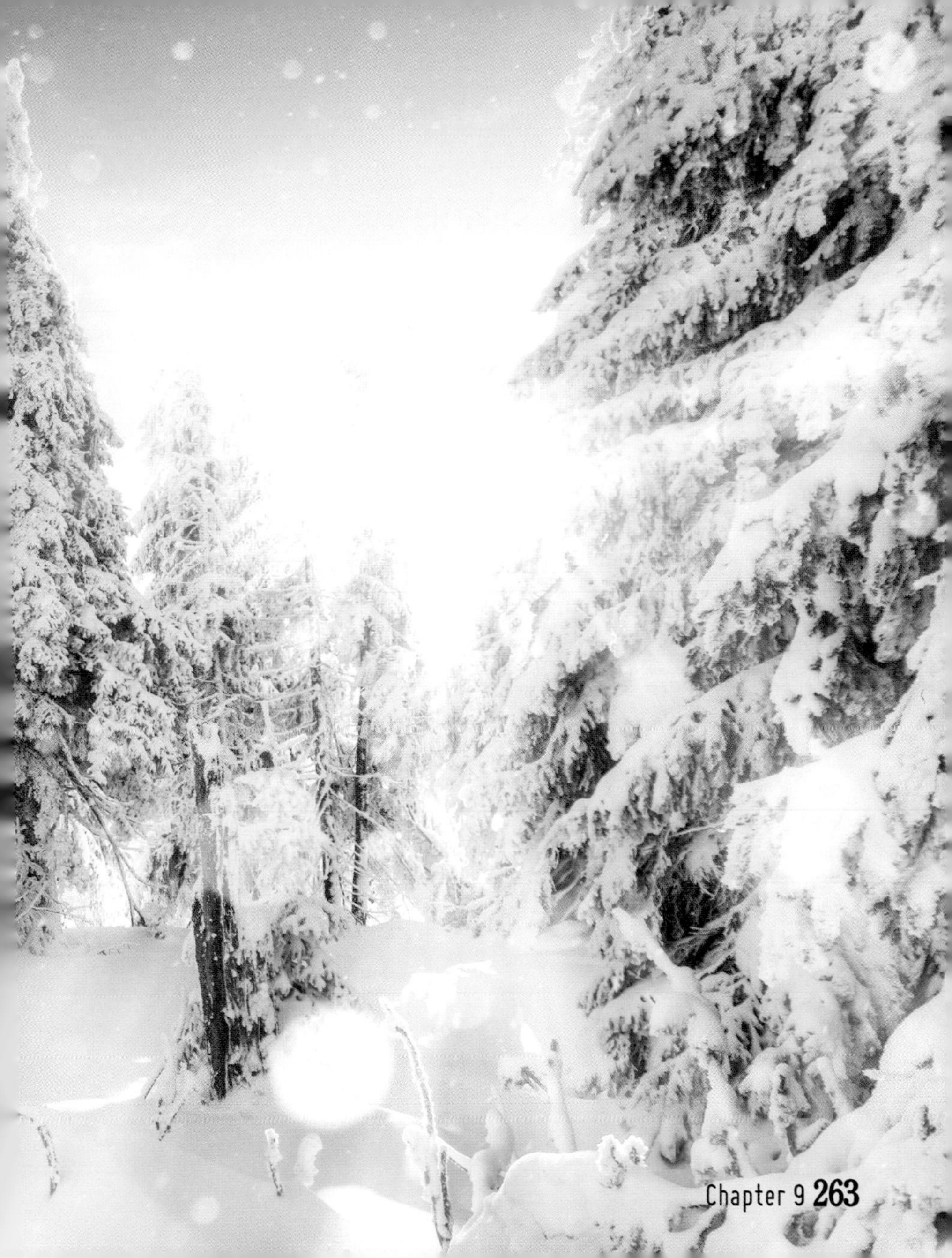

When you were asked to suffer, Lord Jesus, you did so without hesitation. Your courage and your faith inspire me to see my own suffering in a different light. I still do not like it nor wish it to continue, but because of your example, I can handle it with courage, grace, and the knowledge that my hardships are part of your plan for my life. You did not back down in the face of fear, and like you, I hope to find the strength to face my fears, move through them, and come out on the other side with a new sense of hope and possibility. Amen.

> *We can give our burdens to the Lord because he truly understands our pain.*

Dear Lord, you told your followers that they could cast their burdens upon you and that you would take their suffering away. I suffer now and ask that you take this burden from me and bring some relief from the pain and confusion that now fill my life. I know that I'm only so strong and that your strength can help me move past these difficult circumstances and see the goodness in my life again. Take my burden and let me cast my cares upon you, Lord. Help me carry on and get through. Amen.

*H*eavenly Father, how can I come to you with my problems when there are so many people who are suffering far more than I am? I feel needy and selfish, but I don't know where to turn or how to deal with things the way they are. I ask in prayer that you show me some light upon which I can focus my heart and my hope — light that will lead me forward through the darkness knowing that on the other side of suffering there will be eternal joy. Lord, please hear my prayer.

*A*nd he said to them all, If any man will come after me, let him deny himself, and take up his cross daily, and follow me. For whosoever will save his life shall lose it: but whosoever will lose his life for my sake, the same shall save it. — Luke 9:23–24

*D*ear God, how blessed I am to have someone who understands the deepest part of me. No matter what I'm feeling or going through, you know my heart and all of its shadows. Your wisdom is always exactly what I need to hear and when I need to hear it, and your comfort shields me from the cold and the dark. I find hope and courage and a sense of purpose in you that keeps me going even when my days are filled with chaos and disorder. Thank you for truly understanding me.

Blessed are ye, when men shall hate you, and when they shall separate you from their company, and shall reproach you, and cast out your name as evil, for the Son of man's sake. Rejoice ye in that day, and leap for joy: for, behold, your reward is great in heaven: for in the like manner did their fathers unto the prophets. — Luke 6:22–23

Father God, how your beloved Son, Jesus Christ, must have suffered for us! Yet here we are with our petty complaints about life, not realizing that we could have it much worse. Today I would like to pray for the inner peace that only you can give and for the well-being of others. I'm grateful to know that I can overcome anything with your love, God, but now I would like to assure others of that same love, which is available to them anytime they go to you and ask for it. May they be brought back home to you in faith.

*L*ord God, I pray to you today for a little bit of grace in handling the challenges of my life. I've fought intolerance and impatience, and I've grown tired and angry more times than I care to think of. I long for happier, lighter times, but I know that first I must pass through these trials. I pray for grace, and some comfort, too, so that even as I find the inner strength to face what must be faced, I will rest secure in the knowledge that I'm never alone. Thank you, Lord.

Just as the sufferings of Christ flow over into our lives, so also through Christ our comfort overflows to others.

> *And his disciples came to him, and awoke him, saying, Lord, save us, we perish. And he saith unto them, Why are ye fearful, O ye of little faith? Then he arose, and rebuked the wind and the sea; and there was a great calm.* — Matthew 8:25–26

Dear God, you are my comforter and my protector, my refuge and my guide. I look to you for the light that serves to bring me safely home through the high and mighty waves and the great winds. You are the lighthouse upon the shore, and I watch for your light and follow where it leads: directly out of suffering and back into happiness and joy once again. I may always have trials, but I know that I also will always find my way out through your guidance. You are my comforter and my protector, my refuge and my guide.

ather God, you gave us your only begotten Son so that we could learn from his life and his example. I know that suffering is a part of life and that no one is immune, and I'm willing to endure my share of suffering. I only ask that you stand beside me to make sure that I can handle all that is given to me with grace, patience, and kindness. Often when my life is in shambles, I lash out at those closest to me. Help me be more like Jesus, who suffered terribly, yet still loved others with a selfless compassion.

You chose to suffer for my benefit, Lord Jesus, and I thank you with all my heart. On the other hand, I know that my suffering is for my own benefit to help me grow and become a better person. I know that you understand my pain, and knowing that truly comforts me. Just to be heard and understood does a lot to make my troubles worthwhile. Your loving presence continues to provide me with the strength and fortitude I need to keep going down the path you set before me. And I thank you for helping me see the silver lining around each and every cloud.

No one understands my pain like Jesus, who suffered as one of us and came back to comfort us in our sorrows.

God, I can finally see some light at the end of this tunnel. The past few months have been so trying and so difficult, but now I feel my spirit lifting, and my heart is lighter, too. Thank you for being right here with me the whole way, never leaving me even when I complained too much or when I was desperate and doubting. I could not have made it this far without your love, and now I'm looking forward to this new lease on life that you have given me. The suffering was worth the joy of coming through it alive, renewed, and filled with a sense of release. Thank you, God.

It has been a long and trying time, Lord, and I'm more than ready for my burdens to be removed from me. I pray that I can finally embrace whatever lessons there are to be learned and whatever wisdom there is to be gleaned from this situation in my heart and in my mind. I know that we all must have rain in our lives along with the sun, but how I miss the warmth of that sun on my face! I pray that this is the end of my dark nights for a while and that I can enjoy the light of a new day.

Whosoever cometh to me, and heareth my sayings, and doeth them, I will shew you to whom he is like: He is like a man which built an house, and digged deep, and laid the foundation on a rock: and when the flood arose, the stream beat vehemently upon that house, and could not shake it: for it was founded upon a rock. — Luke 6:47–48

God, isn't there an easier way to grow as a person? Suffering causes so much pain, and when I'm going through it, I often can't see the end of it. I know that it must be for my own good, but if possible, could you take some of this weight off my shoulders? Just enough so that I can continue onward and upward. I pray for your help today.

Be glad then, ye children of Zion, and rejoice in the Lord your God: for he hath given you the former rain moderately, and he will cause to come down for you the rain, the former rain, and the latter rain in the first month. And the floors shall be full of wheat, and the vats shall overflow with wine and oil. — Joel 2:23–24

Lord Jesus, you are my inspiration and my hope. In you I see what I want to be and how I want to walk through the world. You took your burdens and did not complain. You stood in the face of fear and did not let it overwhelm you. You held your ground and did not compromise your integrity and values, even when doing so might have saved you from suffering. I look to you as a model of the kind of person I hope to become. Mold and shape me into your image, Lord. Amen.

*D*ear Lord, show me the way out of my suffering. I'm not asking that you take it away from me, only that you show me how I can survive it with my head and my heart intact. I know that you suffered, and by your experience and wisdom I hope to be able to rise to my challenges and learn what you have to teach me. I know this is a trial by fire, and with you by my side I'm not afraid of being burned...I only want to be made righteous in Christ. Amen.

> *Christ suffered for you so that you should follow in his steps. Therefore, I have faith knowing God feels and shares all my burdens and trials.*

*I*s there a purpose to my misery, God? Is there a point to my pain and suffering? I long to know the purpose. I want to trust that your will is at work here in my life. I suppose all I can do is keep surrendering and letting it all go so that you can best handle the situations that I cannot. But this takes a lot of faith, God! So please deepen my faith in you to do for me what might seem impossible right now in the midst of my hurt and anger. It's hard to completely let go, but I'm doing that now in prayer. Thank you, God, for handling my problems and carrying my burdens.

When will I learn, Lord, that some temptations are best left alone? I know in my head that my suffering comes from giving into temptations, but my head isn't always in charge of my heart or my thoughts, it seems. Please help me have the inner strength and the integrity to avoid as much negative temptation as possible. And when I do give in and get hurt, help me have the faith and the courage to learn from my mistakes and accept responsibility for my actions. I may not be perfect, but I'm trying, Lord!

I will sing of the mercies of the Lord for ever: with my mouth will I make known thy faithfulness to all generations. For I have said, Mercy shall be built up for ever: thy faithfulness shalt thou establish in the very heavens.

— Psalm 89:1–2

O God, it helps so much to know that whatever I'm feeling, you are feeling it too, and that whatever suffering I'm asked to deal with, you are dealing with it too. I feel as though I have a constant and loving parent watching over me at all times, looking out for me. Sensing your presence makes me feel stronger and more confident about my place in the world. Thank you for your presence and your power in my life. I recognize that you are always with me, even in the bad times, for it is then that my heart seeks you the most.

Christ, help me have the same faith that you had when you were called upon to face your fears. Help me have the same strength that you had when you were called upon to resist temptation. Help me have the same courage you showed when dealing with those who wanted to do you harm. By your perfect example, I hope to live an exemplary life. With you as my inspiration, I hope to one day inspire others to follow the same path you have laid out for me. Lord, please help me be as much like you as I humanly can. I pray in your name. Amen.

*A*nd whosoever doth not bear his cross, and come after me, cannot be my disciple. For which of you, intending to build a tower, sitteth not down first, and counteth the cost, whether he have sufficient to finish it?

— Luke 14:27–28

Jesus understands our every weakness because he was tempted in the same ways that we are tempted.

orgive me, God, for my weaknesses and insecurities. Please shower me with mercy and grace when I come up short or fail to live up to your righteous standard. I pray to you today so that I might know your presence more deeply and make better decisions that more accurately reflect your will for my life. I may sometimes do the wrong thing, but with your love and kindness and compassion, I know that I can be more obedient and do what is right. I may not often act as maturely as I would like, but with your patience, I'm learning more and more each day. Thank you, God, for your mercy, your grace, your patience, and your forgiveness.

*D*ear Father, sometimes I forget how blessed I am. I forget to be grateful. I forget to be patient. I forget to be kind. I forget that suffering is something we all must go through, and that our attitude determines how we come out of it. I ask that you help me slow down enough to see just how good life is, even when things appear to be not so good on the outside. Help me see the silver linings around each cloud. Life can be hard, but if I keep my eyes on you, it is worth every moment.

*W*here there is suffering, Lord, let me be a beacon of hope for others. Where there is pain, let me somehow find a way to comfort those who can't comfort themselves. Where there is violence, let me be the calm that helps restore harmony. Where there is anguish, let me be a soothing balm. I have been blessed with good times and bad, and I know that the bad have been just as important to my growth as the good. So now, Lord, let me help others who have not yet come to understand your deep workings in their lives. Where there is confusion, let me be clarity. Use me, Lord, in any way you can today and every day of my life.

Chapter 10

The Lord Strengthens Our Faith

Dear heavenly Father, you have been my helper, my comfort, my protector, my provider — my everything — for some time now. Because I have come to trust in you, I can't imagine my life without you. Over time, your faithfulness has steadied my faith in you. Your goodness to me has softened my cynicism. Your love has covered my faults. Your salvation has given me a hope and a future. Thank you for leading me along this path of life.

*W*henever I've tried to do things my way, Lord, we've both seen the outcome. I have a long list of failed attempts at self-management. It's through these failures, however, that I've come to understand that your way is best. I don't have the perspective of seeing things from the beginning to the end as you do. And so, whenever I trust in you, listening to you speak to me from your Word and through your Holy Spirit, I don't have to worry about outcomes, because you always bring about what's best for me.

Faith is the foundation upon which a happy, healthy life is built. The stronger our faith, the less our life can be shaken by outside occurrences and extraneous circumstances.

Trust in the Lord, and do good; so shalt thou dwell in the land, and verily thou shalt be fed. Delight thyself also in the Lord: and he shall give thee the desires of thine heart. — Psalm 37:3–4

I remember, almighty God, when my level of trust in you was foolishly small. I had many misconceptions about you, and rumors about what you were like hung in the back of my mind. Were you out to punish me at my first misstep? Are you always angry and difficult to please? Since I placed my life in your hands, was I doomed to a dismal existence? Would you make me suffer continually? I feel kind of ashamed of those awful thoughts now that I know the truth about you. Thank you for your patience and love that have gently led me into a fuller understanding of your goodness and your faithfulness to my total welfare.

$\mathcal{W}$alking with you, dear Lord, has been such a series of pleasant surprises and gifts. It's not that there haven't been hard times, but those hard times would have come into my life anyway. It's your presence, Lord, that has made the difference. I believe I have experienced a multitude of blessings from your hand, but you also have been there with me in every trial, soothing my anguish with your compassion and giving me your strength, courage, and perspective. In good times and bad, you've taught me that I can always count on you being here with me.

It's always something! Life never quits handing out lemons, Lord. Sometimes I foolishly think that the current batch of lemons will hopefully be the last batch I'll get, but then there's the lemon truck pulling into my driveway again. Help me be able to smile whenever those lemons get delivered to my doorstep, knowing that you will show me what I need to do with them. You've helped me every time I've asked you, bringing good out of each bad situation. Thank you, Lord.

> *Faith is the foundation upon which a happy, healthy life is built. The stronger our faith, the less our life can be shaken by outside occurrences and extraneous circumstances.*

Dear heavenly Father, if I had to live my life according to the stock market or the weather, or how my favorite sports team is doing, I'd go crazy. If my happiness or well-being depended on those things, I'd be doomed. I'm so grateful that no matter what is going on around me — what circumstances are shifting under my feet — your grip on my life is firm, never compromised nor changed by anything this life dishes out. Indeed, you are my rock.

What a relief in this throwaway world of ever-changing values to know that God is the same yesterday, today, and tomorrow. He is as sure as a sunrise and a sunset.

$\mathcal{M}$y supreme God, I'm so grateful that I can confidently come to you with anything that is on my heart and mind. I know that you have said in your Word that I can cast all my cares on you, because you care for me, but I didn't always believe that my prayers could include things like the small details of my life or the negative feelings of anger and frustration I sometimes struggle with. Instead, you have taught me that you will always receive me when I come to you. Thank you for being such a compassionate God.

I used to fret, Lord, when people had wrong impressions about me or believed things that weren't true about me. I used to think I had to set the record straight as soon as possible. But you've taught me that, more often than not, it's best to wait and let truth win its own victories over time. You have a way of bringing the truth to light in far better ways than I ever could. So when justice seems far away, and when unfairness and lies surround me, remind me again, Lord, that you will again, as you have done many times before, declare the truth on my behalf.

Commit thy way unto the Lord; trust also in him; and he shall bring it to pass. And he shall bring forth thy righteousness as the light, and thy judgment as the noonday. — Psalm 37:5–6

$\mathcal{S}$adly, God, there have been some foolish things I've trusted in the past! I mean, things I've trusted in ways I should only have trusted you for. I've tried to make gods out of other people, possessions, positions, and power. I shudder to think of my foolishness in putting these things in your place. None of them have proved trustworthy, faithful, or able to help me in times of need, let alone able to love me as you do! I know now that the place reserved only for you in my life will never have a rival. You alone are worthy of my trust and love.

There are many events in our lives over which we have no control. Our trust in God produces the endurance that sees us through the tough times we all face in this life.

> *Among the gods there is none like unto thee, O Lord; neither are there any works like unto thy works. All nations whom thou hast made shall come and worship before thee, O Lord; and shall glorify thy name. For thou art great, and doest wondrous things: thou art God alone.* — Psalm 86:8–10

As I recall the ways you've deepened my faith, God, there are certain faces that come to mind — people you put in my path — people who have a remarkable faith stemming from a vibrant relationship with you. How these people have shaped my understanding of your love and faithfulness! Thank you for each one, for their prayers, for their transparency, for their kindness, and also for their patience with me. I have seen what you are like through them. How blessed I am to have, or have had, each one in my life!

The streams of my heart used to flow in so many different directions, searching for pools of loyalty and love. How often they were emptied into desert sands or stinky swamplands! Disappointment and disillusionment are the bitter pills of youth. But then I encountered the ocean of your love and faithfulness, Lord. What a difference you have made in my life! My whole heart runs as one river now toward you and you alone.

> Teach me thy way, O Lord; I will walk in thy truth: unite my heart to fear thy name. I will praise thee, O Lord my God, with all my heart: and I will glorify thy name for evermore. — Psalm 86:11–12

*A*s we learn to trust God, we discover his strengthening presence in various places and in different people. Whenever we find shelter, comfort, rest, and peace, we are bound to hear his voice, welcoming us.

Thank you for the promises in your Word, Lord, that sustain my faith when the stretch of life's road I'm on seems to pass through a wasteland. As I'm trudging forward, I recall what you have said in the Scriptures, and I'm able to press on. I repeat those lines of vital assurance, and my hope revives. I've learned to cling to your Word when there is nothing else in sight, because I know you do not lie and you will keep every promise you have ever made.

> *A mighty fortress is our God, a bulwark never failing.*
> — Martin Luther

Depression is such a deep pit of the soul, Father in heaven. You have carried me out of that pit more than once, and each time you stayed with me the entire time. Where others could not reach me, you took a hold of me. When others could not understand, you listened and consoled me. While others offered their best advice to no avail, you spoke words of life and healing to me. This is one of many reasons I will never stop praising you, holy Father. How perfect your wisdom is! How great is your steadfast love! You have taught me to trust you, even in the darkest nights of the soul.

I like to recall the ways you have shown your faithfulness to me over time, Lord. I like to think back through the decades and remember the highlights of your steadfast love. There have been the miracles — great and small — of provision, protection, and healing. There have been the divine appointments with people whom you have given me the privilege of helping, and those who have helped me, as well. There have been the timely blessings and encouragements and the gifts of life and love. Since there is so much evidence of your faithfulness to me, I really do have to narrow it down to the highlights. You've blessed me beyond measure!

> *Ah,* what solace there is in God's promise of peace! True help and real peace are to be found in trusting in his guidance and inspiration.

When I lift up faith like a shield in my life, Lord God, when I raise my trust in you at the first sign of trouble, how changed my perspective becomes! I see you standing between me and my challenges; I see you making a way for me to victory; I see your strength and your wisdom coming to my aid. My knees stop knocking together, and my heart is filled with courage. May a song of victorious praise be on my lips today, Lord, as I hold high this faith you have caused to live within me.

God's love is wider than our worries, longer than our loneliness, stronger than our sorrows, deeper than our doubts, and higher than our hostilities. Just as valleys are wide, rivers are long, winds are strong, oceans are deep, and the sky is high, so we can have a picture of the wonder of God's love.

*E*ven when my faith fails, dear God, your love does not. Thank you for holding on to me through thick and thin. When I've felt too weak to hold on to you and have believed that all would be lost in the storm, I've discovered that you always keep me safe in your loving arms. Sheltered and cradled there, I am reassured that nothing can separate me from your love. It's this amazing love of yours that I have come to trust so gratefully.

Stand therefore, having your loins girt about with truth, and having on the breastplate of righteousness; and your feet shod with the preparation of the gospel of peace; above all, taking the shield of faith, wherewith ye shall be able to quench all the fiery darts of the wicked.
— Ephesians 6:14–16

> *As ye have therefore received Christ Jesus the Lord, so walk ye in him, rooted and built up in him, and stablished in the faith, as ye have been taught, abounding therein with thanksgiving.*
> — Colossians 2:6–7

Each day as I walk alongside you, Lord, I learn more about trusting you and about living in this faith you have established in my heart. I pray that these roots of trust will grow strong, deep, and wide and that loving obedience to your voice will flourish as a result. Thank you for speaking to my heart through your Word and by your Spirit, who leads me into all truth. I love this journey of faith: What an adventure! And what a blessing!

*I*t's much easier now to walk in faith than it used to be, heavenly Father. How I used to worry, wondering if you'd come through! Now I just wait for you, knowing it's not a matter of if but when your answer or intervention will come. And I have learned, too, that your timing is flawless. You are never too late, never too early, always on time. And so now, even while everything may look like chaos on the outside, I can be calm on the inside. I can sleep at night and go peacefully through my day because I know you are in control.

Wherein ye greatly rejoice, though now for a season, if need be, ye are in heaviness through manifold temptations, that the trial of your faith, being much more precious than of gold that perisheth, though it be tried with fire, might be found unto praise and honour and glory at the appearing of Jesus Christ. — 1 Peter 1:6–7

The tests of time have strengthened and purified my faith in you, Lord. You have purged away the conditions I used to put on you — all those "Lord, I'll trust you if…" prayers. You've smelted away the doubt that used to set up contingency plans in case you didn't come through for me. You've done away with my reliance on my own understanding for approaching life's challenges. How different my faith looks today because you have patiently and faithfully refined it in your wisdom and love!

> *I'm grateful to the Lord for reaching out and drawing me under his wings. His love is so great that he knows my troubles, is concerned for my welfare, and is working to renew my joy.*

ord, you reveal many pictures of your love for me in the Scriptures. Today I recall the metaphor of a hen gathering her tiny chicks under her wings for protection and warmth, just as you gather those who belong to you under the shelter of your love. My soul can know the contentment of that place of refuge today as I come to you in faith. I hide there, trusting that you care for me and will keep me safely tucked away within the blessing of your tender mercies.

God, not everyone understands and appreciates my faith in you. People sometimes see my waiting on you as passiveness. At other times, they see my boldness in moving forward into the unseen truth of your promises as foolishness. Faith is often the opposite of what a person would naturally be inclined to do, so I understand why they wonder about me. I know it looks funny or strange from the outside, but when your guidance is clear to me on the inside, I can't worry about what others will think. Though I shun public opinion as a means of navigating my life, I pray that you would reveal yourself to those who do not know you yet. May they see the wisdom of your ways as the fruit of my faith ripens before their eyes.

It is grace that brought me safe thus far, and grace will lead me home. — John Newton

Dear Lord, there are those who think there cannot be a God because of the evil in the world. It truly makes me sad that they cannot see the manifold blessings of your benevolence despite the reality of a fallen world. It deeply pains my heart that they cannot trust that you have an ultimate plan for dealing with evil and that you have prepared a way of salvation for any-one who would receive it. How heart-rending it is to know that you extend your love and goodness to them but they cannot perceive it! O Father, help those who desire to have faith but cannot find their way to it. In Jesus' name, I pray. Amen.

> *I will sing of the mercies of the Lord for ever: with my mouth will I make known thy faithfulness to all generations. For I have said, Mercy shall be built up for ever: thy faithfulness shalt thou establish in the very heavens.*
> — Psalm 89:1–2

I want the young people in my life to learn to trust in you, Lord, as you have taught me to do. I pray for them today. I ask that you would reveal yourself to them in ways they can perceive and respond to. I pray that you will find them at times and in places where peer pressure is not tugging at them and when they can stop and listen and know that you are speaking to them, calling to them, and drawing them near. Challenge their faithlessness with your truth and love. Illuminate the reality of life's emptiness without you. May they hunger and thirst for you and find you to be exactly what they have been longing for.

Chapter 11

God Always Keeps His Promises

O God, there are times when I feel as if I don't have a friend in the world — no one who really cares about me or what I'm going through. Everyone I know seems to be too busy with their own lives and their own problems. But I'm so grateful that you are always here with me no matter how often I need you. Your promise of eternal love is my bedrock of strength that helps me get through the challenges of my life, even when those who love me don't have the time or patience to help. Thank you, God, for never abandoning me.

Dear Lord, I pray for release from the pain and suffering I'm going through. I know that you are here with me, watching over me, and that you will never give me something I'm not equipped to handle. I know that I can lean on you when I'm weak and tired and without strength. But I still ask for some relief from my struggles and release from the pain. I put my faith and hope in you to keep the promises you made to me. Lord, please stay with me and don't give up on me.

$\mathcal{W}$e know that there are few greater disappointments than to think no one cares or understands. That is why Jesus' promise of his eternal presence is truly precious to us, for he promised, "Remember, I am with you always, to the end of the age."

*A*nd, Thou, Lord, in the beginning hast laid the foundation of the earth; and the heavens are the works of thine hands. They shall perish; but thou remainest; and they all shall wax old as doth a garment; And as a vesture shalt thou fold them up, and they shall be changed: but thou art the same, and thy years shall not fail. — Hebrews 1:10–12

*H*eavenly Father, how good it is to know that you understand me, even when others don't! I don't have to explain myself to you, because you know my mind, my heart, and my soul. Just having you in my life makes me feel as though I have a companion to walk beside me through sunny fields and dark valleys, a companion who won't run off and leave me at the first sign of trouble. Your steadfast love is what keeps me strong. How good it is to know you are always with me!

It took me a long time to get here, Lord — to a place where I have total faith in you. I fought and resisted you every step of the way, but when I finally realized that you never failed to keep the promises you made to me, I also realized that you would never harm or abandon me. My faith in you has become my fortress and my freedom, for I know that I don't have to fight and resist you any longer. I can enjoy my life and relax in the understanding that no matter what happens, you are here with me. Amen.

Faithfulness comes from a God who has kept and is in the process of fulfilling every promise revealed in Scriptures. We are commanded to have faith in God, and out of that faith flows our ability to keep the promises we have made as husbands and wives, as children, as parents, and as servants of God.

My brethren, count it all joy when ye fall into divers temptations. Knowing this, that the trying of your faith worketh patience. But let patience have her perfect work, that ye may be perfect and entire, wanting nothing.

— James 1:2–4

As your beloved child, Father in heaven, I place my hope and my faith entirely in you and your will for my life. In the Scriptures, I'm told that your love for me never ends, even upon death. And so, I surrender to your will and your guidance, knowing that as I continue to serve you, I will continue to be blessed with your loving presence. My faith in you helps me have faith in myself, and in others, too. Blessings abound, Father, when I place my hope and my faith entirely in you!

Sometimes I get the feeling, God, that I'm all alone in this world. Things go wrong, and I can't find the right solutions. People react in ways I can't control or predict. I just feel as though there's no point or purpose to it all. Please help me find a deeper truth about life, a truth that will get me through the confusing and frustrating times when nothing seems to go my way. Help me understand that it all happens for a reason and that the reason is your will for me. I know your will is the promise of a better life; I just need your help to remain steadfast in my faith in you.

Every man also to whom God hath given riches and wealth, and hath given him power to eat thereof, and to take his portion, and to rejoice in his labour; this is the gift of God. For he shall not much remember the days of his life; because God answereth him in the joy of his heart. — Ecclesiastes 5:19–20

You know in your hearts and souls, all of you, that not one thing has failed of all the good things that the Lord your God promised concerning you; all have come to pass for you, not on of them has failed. — Joshua 23:14

Which way do I go, Lord? What choice do I make? I'm told in the Bible that your thoughts are higher than my thoughts and that your will is greater than my will. I come to you in prayer for signs of the direction you wish me to take and the choices you wish me to make. Your promises of everlasting love and life give me faith and hope, but it's the guidance I often seem to lack. Help me focus on the little signs you give me each day, so that my path takes me to that higher place you have promised me. Thank you, Lord, for answering my prayer.

Dear Lord, you never fail to amaze me with the miracles you bless me with each day. I'm not talking about big, spectacular miracles, but those little things that remind me you care about me. My family, my friends, my work, the beautiful things I own — they are all reminders of your love for me, your cherished child. But even if I had no material possessions, Lord, I would still know that you loved me, because you gave me life, as well as the fulfillment of a promise to always walk with me throughout my life. I'm blessed and loved, and that is all I need to feel joy in my heart and happiness in my soul.

*Ch*oosing to live as a people of hope is not to diminish or belittle pain and suffering or to ignore evil's reality. Instead, we cling to God's promise that he will make all things new.

God, your promise to make all things new is what I need right now. There seems to be so much old stuff clogging up my life and making my progress difficult if not impossible. I know that a snake must shed its skin now and then, and though I'm not a snake, it feels as if I can't get the old skin off and let the new skin out. Will you help me have the patience and the faith that all of these blocks will be removed one day and that the old will indeed give way to the new? I look forward with joyful expectation of those new days ahead, but I wish they would come faster.

Dear Lord, I know there is bad and evil in this world. I see it all around me on the news and in my own life. But that does not stop me from clinging fast to my faith in you and to my hope that there is a place beyond this life where evil does not exist. I trust in your promises of heaven and of eternal love, and I know that if I keep my hope alive, I will one day see that promise fulfilled. It does get hard, when pain and suffering are so close at hand, but your presence is the light of hope that guides me through the darkest of dark days. Thank you, Lord.

> *N*ow is my soul troubled; and what shall I say? Father, save me from this hour: but for this cause came I unto this hour. Father, glorify thy name. Then came there a voice from heaven, saying, I have both glorified it, and will glorify it again. — John 12:27–28

In the middle of the night, when all is dark and frightening, the only thing I have to hold onto, precious Lord, is the promise of the coming dawn. When my life is like the long, dark night, I hold onto you and your love. I know that if I can just make it through the hours before daybreak, I will be rewarded with the joy and warmth that a new sunrise can bring. As these long hours of night pass slowly by and I wait for the first light of morning, help me hold fast to you, Lord, as my hope and salvation.

*T*oday is a day for celebration, God, for all the wonderful gifts you have given me through your love and faith in me. The promise of your constant presence is a reason for singing out in joy and praise and in gratitude for blessings big and small. No matter what the new day ahead of me might bring, I know I'm not alone in this thing called life. You are here, ready to take up my cause at any time, and you are always on standby should I need you. Thank you, God, for being here with me and for never failing to fulfill your promises to me.

> *God's love is true and is always reaching out to us. His faithful love is cause for celebration.*

The Lord is thy keeper. The Lord is thy shade upon thy right hand. The sun shall not smite thee by day, nor the moon by night. The Lord shall preserve thee from all evil. He shall preserve thy soul. The Lord shall preserve thy going out and thy coming in from this time forth, and even for evermore. — Psalm 121:5–8

There are no sure things in life and no guarantees of happiness and joy, except when I turn to you, O God, for you alone are a sure thing and a guarantee of a life filled with love and peace and the kind of confidence that goes far beyond my outer achievements. With you, God, there may still be sad days to experience, but having you here beside me, urging me to carry on through the pain, makes me understand that there is a reason, a purpose, and a time for all things under heaven. You alone are my sure thing, God.

*L*ord Jesus, you suffered so I could benefit from your pain, your experience, and your devotion to God. No matter how much you feared your destiny, you walked toward it with courage and the understanding that God would fulfill his promises to you. Now, help me do the same by overcoming my fears while knowing that the fulfillment of your promises to me lies waiting around the bend. I may not see the path ahead of me, but I can still step out in faith knowing with a full heart that you are walking beside me, ready to hold me up if I should stumble and fall. That was your promise to me, and I'm deeply grateful, Lord. Amen.

Faith is more than believing in who God is. It's believing that he will keep his promises.

And the prayer of faith shall save the sick, and the Lord shall raise him up; and if he have committed sins, they shall be forgiven him. Confess your faults one to another, and pray one for another, that ye may be healed. The effectual fervent prayer of a righteous man *availeth much.* — James 5:15–16

My friends tell me I have to have faith and "let go and let God," and yet when I try to let go, I feel resistance within me. It has always been hard for me to trust anyone, and yet I'm alive and well and that should be enough for me to trust in you, God. I pray today for a stronger faith and for the courage to give up control of my life to you. I pray for the ability to just surrender it all and let your Holy Spirit move me, instead of me always trying to figure it all out for myself. Help me have faith in you, God, and in your will for me.

Lord, please take away my anxieties and my worries about tomorrow, and please let me rest awhile in the present moment. I spend so much time either regretting the past or completely stressing out over what might happen tomorrow that I forget the gift of the present and the awareness of your presence in my life. Only in the quiet and calm of the moment at hand can I sense that you are with me. Sometimes I forget you in the busyness of my life, and that is when my anxiety returns. Help me, Lord, to stay in the present and in that wonderful place of peace and calm where I can listen to your voice.

> Let us know the truth of His promise: that the whole world may not be able to take away His peace.
> — Søren Kierkegaard

> *Therefore being justified by faith, we have peace with God through our Lord Jesus Christ, by whom also we have access by faith into this grace wherein we stand, and rejoice in hope of the glory of God.*
> — Romans 5:1–2

Heavenly Father, give me the peace that passes all understanding, a peace so deep that no matter what storms blow into my life I stand secure upon the foundation of my faith in you. Give me a peace that accompanies me along even the scariest roads of life, telling me that I have all the courage and strength I need to handle anything that crosses my path. Give me a peace that soothes my heart when it is broken and calms my spirit when it is out of harmony and balance. Give me your peace, dear Father, for that is all I need. Amen.

In the midst of my sorrow, I cried great tears of joy because of his priceless promise that he never wastes our pain. On the other side of this trial, I know for certain that I will see his purpose fulfilled, and as always, I will find reasons to celebrate.

Dear Jesus, your promise of mercy and grace is cause for rejoicing. I long to show others just how much you have done for me and how your promises of eternal life and love have lifted me up from the dark places in my life. May I be a vessel of your love, pouring it out to others, and may I proclaim your good words and deeds so that those I come in contact with can see how much you have transformed my life. I want to celebrate this special relationship I have with you.

*I*t is one thing, O God, to tell the people in my life about all the wondrous miracles you've performed for me. But when they see the light in my eyes and feel the uplifting joy of my spirit, those things speak far more than words ever could. Your promise of unceasing love and concern for me shines through me like a beacon, attracting others to me. They want to know my secret of happiness, and I tell them there is no secret but you, dear God, at work in my life in the most mysterious of ways. May I be your light in the world to all who may need a way out of darkness.

> *W*hen outward strength is broken, faith rests on the promises. In the midst of sorrow, faith draws the sting out of every trouble, and takes out the bitterness from every affliction. — Robert Cecil

Chapter 12

The Lord Cares for Us

Sometimes, heavenly Father, I hear people talk about your love as if it were a consolation prize, a last resort, or a lackluster alternative to human love and acceptance. Oh, what a mistaken perspective we sometimes have of your tremendous love for us! Your love is deep and unshakable, faithful and far-reaching. It picks us up out of the depths when we are at our worst and then flings wide the door of acceptance when we return home to you. Your love is here when everyone else has gone away, and it waits for us when we wander off after fickle and false loves. Your love is the best prize among all prizes, and I value it above all other things.

$\mathcal{I}$t's a strange reality, Lord Jesus, the connection between suffering and love. When we needed to be rescued from evil, you endured great suffering for our sakes, and when we needed to be cleansed from our sins, you died so that we could become pure before God — and you did all this because you loved us so deeply. Mothers suffer through childbirth because of a powerful maternal love. Fathers sacrifice themselves in service to their families, sometimes working multiple jobs to provide shelter, food, and clothing for their family because of love. Remind me today, Lord, that my suffering doesn't have to be meaningless. I can offer it up to you, drawing near to your love, becoming more loving and compassionate toward others who suffer, and sharing in the fellowship of your sufferings.

For I am persuaded, that neither death, nor life, nor angels, nor principalities, nor powers, nor things present, nor things to come, nor height, nor depth, nor any other creature, shall be able to separate us from the love of God, which is in Christ Jesus our Lord.
— Romans 8:38–39

How deep will the pain go? Rest assured, never deeper than the Lord's love.

My trials are many, Lord God, and my faith grows weak. I pray today for a stronger faith in your will and your purpose. I surrender to the timing of your grace, knowing that it may not arrive when I want it to, but it will arrive when I need it to. I ask for continued guidance and wisdom, dear Lord, so that I can overcome these trials to the best of my ability. I ask for your mercy so that these trials may never become anything I can't handle. Most of all, I ask that you remain beside me as my companion, my inspiration, and my friend.

think our culture often makes a caricature of love, heavenly Father. We think of love in terms of hearts and teddy bears, chocolates and flowers, romances and Norman Rockwell moments. But when I look at your best expression of love — your Son, Jesus — my common notions of love are swept away. In him, I see the Wonderful Counselor speaking truth, whether it was good news or uncomfortable realities. I see the Mighty God walking in gentle humility, stooping to serve us. I see the Everlasting Father reaching down in empathy to offer salvation to a stubbornly self-sufficient humanity. And I see the Prince of Peace entering our chaos and offering his own self to bring the peace our souls so desperately need. Please fill my heart and mind with this kind of love, Father.

I know, O Lord, that thy judgments are right, and that thou in faithfulness hast afflicted me. Let, I pray thee, thy merciful kindness be for my comfort, according to thy word unto thy servant. — Psalm 119:75–76

How long wilt thou forget me, O Lord? for ever? how long wilt thou hide thy face from me? How long shall I take counsel in my soul, having sorrow in my heart daily? how long shall mine enemy be exalted over me?

— Psalm 13:1–2

$\mathcal{P}$ride is the culprit behind my sinful ways, Lord. In my prideful moments, I think I know better than you do, or I think I can give truth the slip and make something work that I know isn't right. But these are foolish thoughts and ways! Wrong can never be right, and your wisdom is perfect. Please forgive me for my arrogance, Lord, in trying to do things my own way and in defying your way of truth and righteousness. Thank you for holding me to the truth and for faithfully correcting me and loving me enough to discipline me. Thank you for your "tough love."

I like to ponder your creation, my Creator God, to wonder at its beauty and complexity. I like to be outdoors and let my senses take in the world you have made. I like to watch and listen to nature programs and learn new things about the wonders of your workmanship. Your Word tells me that you made them in wisdom. There is no doubt! Thank you for these sacred gifts. I truly cherish each one of them.

$\mathcal{M}$orning reminds me, Lord, that the darkness of night is temporary. Sunrise proclaims the promise that there is a dawning of salvation from each sorrow and each pain for those who trust in you. Whether or not we experience that dawning in this life, we know there is an ultimate dawning of eternal freedom from all suffering and sorrow when the line you have drawn on the horizon of time is made bright at your appearing.

Your love is an anchor for my soul, Lord Jesus. The assurance that you love me gives me a focus when nothing seems to make any sense. It calms me when I fear the worst. It keeps me from despairing when I feel like a failure. In every circumstance, I need only recall the reality of your unfailing love, and that is more than enough to hold me steady and give me the peace I need. Thank you, Jesus.

I will be glad and rejoice in thy mercy: for thou hast considered my trouble; thou hast known my soul in adversities; and hast not shut me up into the hand of the enemy. Thou hast set my feet in a large room.

— Psalm 31:7–8

Dear Lord, I think of how you have helped me so many times and in so many ways — how consistently you've loved me and brought me through hardships. I could write a book about it! And then, as if saving me is not enough, you bless me with good things. Your love gifts come in countless forms, and I know I take them for granted too often. But that doesn't seem to stop you from graciously giving them anyway. I just wanted to "notice" the blessings of your love in my life today. I want to give you praise for your steadfast love.

> For God so loved the world, that he gave his only begotten Son, that whosoever believeth in him should not perish, but have everlasting life. For God sent not his Son into the world to condemn the world; but that the world through him might be saved. — John 3:16–17

*L*et each wreath, heavenly Father, be a reminder of your perfect love for me. Let the circle remind me that your love has no beginning or end. Let the evergreen boughs remind me that you came to give me eternal life. Let the red ribbon put me in mind of the gift of your Son and his sacrifice. Let the pine cones remind me to spread the seed of your love by proclaiming the gospel of your salvation. Thank you, Father, for this meaningful way to remember your faithful love during the Christmas season.

For just a moment, Lord Jesus, I want to pull away from the hubbub of Christmas and send you a Valentine message. I love you. I truly do. And I can love you because you first loved me. Without your love, I would not have learned what true love is. So I just wanted to say thank you for loving me first and for show- ing me how to love you back. It never gets old — your love for me — and I never get tired of telling you how much your love means to me.

> *Beneath the supporting hands of friends and helpers, we feel God's strong grasp, and we hold on, no longer alone.*

God, how I enjoy sitting in a darkened room with no lights on except for the Christmas tree lights. Whether silence prevails or Christmas hymns play softly, I feel a sense of reverent peace as I worship you. In those sacred moments, I bring my heart to you, offering my grateful homage in response to your amazing love. How I long to remain near to you as the season moves toward its crescendo! Hold me in this place of peace within, no matter what's transpiring without.

Do you never tire of my coming to you, Lord God? Don't you grow weary when I always have another thing to ask? Do you really not mind my always pondering things in your presence? I get tired of myself sometimes, so it seems incredible that you would continually welcome me without wanting a break from my company. But I'm glad your invitation remains open to me. Your love is beyond comprehension. It stands in stark contrast to my human limitations and failings when it comes to relationships and loving other people. So please help me to learn from your love, to grow in it, and then to pass it on to others. Thank you, Lord, for your continuous presence in my life! I pray with an open heart. Amen.

Lord Jesus, you knew we'd never be able to merit your grace. And so, in love, you took the initiative to save us. Thank you for your proactive love that doesn't wait to receive before it gives. Thank you for your zealous love that charges forward into our apathy and self-centeredness. Thank you for your steadfast love that just doesn't give up. Thank you for loving me with such a great love as you revealed on the cross.

I can run from your love, heavenly Father, and I may even succeed in rejecting it for a time, but you will never stop offering it to me. I think of the prodigal's father, who waited and watched in hope for the safe return of his wayward son. You are that Father who never withdraws his love, no matter the insult or injury to himself. Yours is the noblest of loves, a self-sacrificing love, a beautiful love to behold, and the best love to be held by.

> *But God commendeth his love toward us, in that, while we were yet sinners, Christ died for us.*
>
> — Romans 5:8

In this world where human love is conditional and often temporary, it is a joy to know that God loves us unconditionally and eternally. Nothing we can say or do will cause God to stop loving us.

The changing seasons, my Creator, remind me of your faithful love. For countless generations, these yearly cycles have cued our planting, growing, harvesting, and resting. In your wisdom, you've made a proper time for everything. In your love, you have created us to understand and enjoy your design in the seasonal variations. How blessed I feel to live in your amazing world and to see your love displayed in its wonders!

$\mathcal{Y}$our love does not spare me from every difficulty, Lord, but in your love, you are with me through each difficult thing I face and with each step I take. Your love does not make my pain nonexistent in this life, but your love sustains me as I go through the pain. And with each hardship you carry me through, you remind me of your promise of a future in which none of these trials will find me ever again. Lord, I trust your love enough to know that this hope is sure and that my future with you in paradise is secure.

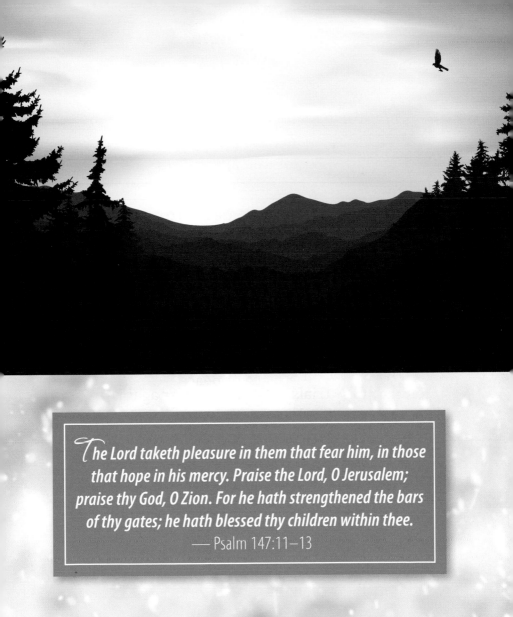

The Lord taketh pleasure in them that fear him, in those that hope in his mercy. Praise the Lord, O Jerusalem; praise thy God, O Zion. For he hath strengthened the bars of thy gates; he hath blessed thy children within thee.

— Psalm 147:11–13

Heavenly Father, please forgive me for expecting others to love me perfectly. (Truly, only you can love me that way.) Indeed, at times I fail to love others as I should. Help me let others off the hook when their love lets me down. Please grant me a heart to forgive, just as you have forgiven me. I don't want old hurts and grudges — or new ones, for that matter — to stand in the way of a truly blessed Christmas celebration. Instead, I pray that the reality of imperfect human love would remind me of why I need your love so much.

> May you be assured of God's presence as you weather this current storm. As the waves toss you about, and the ship of your life threatens to crash into rough rocks: He is there. Never despair. After all, he created all these things, and in him alone they have their existence.

My affections come and go; sometimes I'm more loving, sometimes less. But your love, dear God, is steadfast. Your Word says that your love for me never ceases and that your mercies for me are renewed each morning. I don't deserve your abundance of love and mercy, but you give it to me freely and willingly. Truly, I receive your love gratefully. Only let me not stop there; help me offer that kind of steadfast love to those around me, whether they deserve it or not. Let your love flow through me so that there will be a continuity of true loving kindness at work in my life, ministering to others, regardless of my mood or circumstances.

*A*nticipation is delightful now that I've become an adult, Lord. And yet, I remember how painful it was when I was a child at Christmas time. Oh, the agony of waiting to find out what was in that package with my name on it! It reminds me of how anxious I used to be waiting for your answers, waiting for you to come through for me, and waiting to see if you'd really help me. Thankfully, it's different now. Waiting is not the hand-wringing trial it used to be. Now I can relax even while outcomes are unknown to me because I know that you love me, that you are with me, and that you have my life under control.

Ye, being rooted and grounded in love, may be able to comprehend with all saints what is the breadth, and length, and depth, and height, and to know the love of Christ, which passeth knowledge, that ye might be filled with all the fulness of God. — Ephesians 3:17–19